Claddings
of buildings
Revised edition

Alan J. Brookes

D1417882

Longman
Scientific &
Technical

Longman Scientific & Technical
Longman Group UK Limited,
Longman House, Burnt Mill, Harlow,
Essex CM20 2JE, England
and Associated Companies throughout the world.

© Construction Press 1983
This edition © Longman Group UK Limited 1990

First published 1983
Revised edition 1990
Second impression 1992

British Library Cataloguing in Publication Data
Brooke, Alan J.
 Claddings of buildings. – Student ed.
 1. Building components: claddings
 I. Title
 693

ISBN 0-582-06381-7

Produced by Longman Singapore Publishers Pte Ltd
Printed in Singapore

Contents

iii

Acknowledgements

The notion of writing a book on lightweight claddings in buildings came while working with Scott, Brownrigg & Turner under the guidance of John Church and K. E. Gilham on the early stages of the design for a cladding system at Heathrow Terminal 4.

My lecture notes for B. Arch part I (fourth year) students at the Liverpool School of Architecture were the basis for much of the material contained in the following chapters, and my thanks go to the many students and colleagues who contributed to this course and commented on drafts of the manuscript.

Some of the material has already been used as part of the *Architects' Journal* 'Products in Practice' and 'Art of Construction' series and my thanks go to my colleagues, Martyn Ward and David Yeomans, who helped with this series and to Tim Sage and Barry Evans for their excellent technical editorship of those articles.

Many manufacturers have given helpful advice with the various chapters. In particular I would like to thank Mr Spence and Mr Scott of Empire Stone; Jim Leadbetter of Anmac; the Cem-Fil team at Pilkington; Jim Muir of Plannja Dobel; Alan Ward of H. H. Robertson; Mr Siedentopf of Josef Gartner and to the many others who provided drawings or photographs. I thank all these and the following who have assisted me in various ways: Chris Wilkinson, Brian Taggart, Frank Jones, Dave King, Don Reynolds, Gordon Smith. The excellent artwork was prepared by Ed Robson and Tony Flannery of the Liverpool School of Architecture and I am also grateful to other students, including Dave Cousans, Pat Sheldon and Mike Wigmore, for their permission to reproduce drawings and photographs.

Invaluable help with the photographs came from T. McCooey and I. Hunter. My thanks go to Vera Doud for all her hard work in typing the manuscript. I am also grateful to the staff at Longman, and to Colin Bassett.

Finally, I owe a great debt to Jackie and my three children, Nicholas, Sarah and James, for their help and encouragement during the preparation of this book.

Introduction

'I find it incredible that there will not be a sweeping revolution in the methods of building during the next century. The erection of a house wall, come to think of it, is an astonishingly tedious and complex business: the final result is exceedingly unsatisfactory.'

H. G. Wells (1902)

Non-loadbearing claddings in building, often in panel form, are most commonly used in conjunction with a structural framework. Before considering the six main types of cladding systems in detail we should first briefly examine two concepts which have most closely influenced the development of these types of construction.

Firstly, there was the development of frame construction, and secondly, the introduction of systems of prefabrication, whereby component parts of a building could be fabricated in a builder's yard or workshop prior to their assembly on an actual building site.

The frame

The first building with a skeleton of wrought iron was the Menier chocolate factory near Paris, built 1871/72, where the external skin acts purely as a non-loadbearing panel infill. However, it was in Chicago in the latter part of the nineteenth century that the steel frame building acquired a dominant position in the growth of ideas about panel and frame construction.

The use of the frame offered two main advantages. Firstly, the potential for more square footage per floor area over masonry construction. As much as one floor in a ten-storey block could be saved by the use of a frame. Secondly, the whole weight of the building could be carried on the frame, and by reducing the self-weight of the skin the load on the foundations could be lessened.

This combination of advantages led to the intensive development of the Chicago skyscraper with such examples as the first Leiter building in 1879 and Louis Sullivan's Carson, Pirie, Scott department store of 1899/1904 with its façade of an exposed grid of steel with large glazed infill panels. Subsequent developments have now led to a position where as Colin Rowe (1956) comments:

> The frame has been the catalyst of an architecture, but one might notice that it has also become architecture, that contemporary architecture is almost inconceivable in its absence.

Prefabrication

Examples of industrialisation and prefabrication had occurred all through the nineteenth century, culminating in the spectacular Crystal Palace building for the London Great Exhibition of 1851. Russell (1981) has shown how, following the Battle of Trafalgar in 1805, the mechanised blockmaking plant at the Royal Naval Dockyard at Portsmouth heralded the introduction of machine tools for prefabrication. Herbert (1978) in his excellent study of pioneers of prefabrication gives an early example in the John Manning portable colonial cottage in 1833, using a timber frame with interchangeable timber panels, all designed for ease of erection. Pressure of prefabrication implied the use of some sort of panel system. Beginning in the twentieth century, prefabrication exploited new techniques and materials. In addition to timber, corrugated metal and cast iron, precast concrete emerged as a new system of building with an enormous potential for prefabrication.

Knowledge of new materials

As early as 1905, J. A. Brodie, city engineer of Liverpool, built a three-storey block of flats using the principle of the 'dove-tailed box' with panels cast off-site including apertures for doors and windows. Russell (1981) also reports on what must be the first example of sandwich panels in precast concrete at Watergraafsmeer Garden City, Amsterdam, designed by D. Greiner and built during 1922–24 as part of an experiment to encourage innovative methods in the face of rapidly increasing brick prices. The cladding consisted of an outer layer of concrete, a layer of insulation and an inner layer of lightweight concrete. It may seem surprising, therefore, that the first real guidance on the design of precast concrete was not published until 40 years later (see for example Morris, 1966) when, following the rush to promote and develop housing systems in the 1950s and early 1960s, guidance from the Cement and Concrete Association became widely available. But this is a familiar story in the building industry where general acceptability of new techniques occurs slowly and where established texts on building technology tend to be mainly concerned with traditional forms of construction.

Experience has shown that with the use of relatively untried components and techniques, the architect can no longer rely on the traditional means of communication between design and production. In these circumstances architects may have leaned too heavily on manufacturers' expertise of building construction, not realising that the quality control procedures on-site are often insufficient for the site agent to check that components have been correctly installed.

Changes in scale of use of materials can create problems of their own. For example, characteristics of manufacture and behaviour in use of terracotta tiles were well known in Europe at the turn of the century. Even so, failures occurred due to inadequate provision for thermal expansion and contraction processes when these were applied to tall framed buildings in the USA. These failures are only now becoming obvious and it is interesting to reflect that at such buildings as Atlanta City Hall and the Woolworth building, New York, the original terracotta is now being replaced with another innovative material, precast concrete reinforced with fibreglass. When specifying new materials we are today able to take advantage of research and development techniques, accelerated testing, etc., and more accurately predict their performance in use. Even so, it takes time for the results of this research to filter into common use. Also, in the building industry it is often difficult to carry out sufficient tests to predict accurately the possibility of failure.

In some cases architects may be wary of using a material due to past experience with similar products. For example, most architects respect the corrosion of metals, and until better means of protection became available there was a general reluctance to use metal panels in building. Thus although techniques for shaping metals were sufficiently well known in 1932 for the development of lightweight metal cladding panels, as used by Jean Prouvé at the Roland Garros Aviation Club building, it was not until much later (Wachsmann, 1961; Sebestyen, 1977) that the principles of design were discussed in detail, and then with little reference to Prouvé.

In general, architects feel a responsibility towards their clients and are reluctant to use a material until it is well tried and tested. This may explain why it was not until the mid 1950s, with the Monsanto 'House of the Future' at Disneyland, that serious investigation of moulded plastics as building panels began, although a survey, published by the *Architects' Journal* (1942), of possible future applications of plastics for the industry reported on building units of comparatively large size being made by a number of moulding methods ten years earlier. Even so, it was not until conferences such as one organised by the University of Surrey in 1974 that advice on the design and specification of glass reinforced polyester (GRP) cladding became widely available.

In some instances there is almost an irrational resistance to the use of a particular material. Pilkington Bros. have obviously seen the need to establish the credibility of a relatively new material like glass reinforced cement by issuing comprehensive design guidance on its use. Even so, architects, perhaps affected by experience in the development of high alumina cement, were over-cautious about such factors as the durability of the material. There is still a need for feedback from the performance of glass fibre reinforced cement (GRC) of products in use.

Changes in use for different building types and markets can also influence architects' attitudes towards a material. Technical guidance on asbestos cement, aluminium and steel profiled cladding was hardly thought necessary when its use was restricted to industrial sheds. Architects relied entirely on the technical literature produced by the various manufacturers, which although generally very comprehensive did not always show the material in relation to others. It was not until the 1970s that comprehensive guidance on profiled cladding was available from the Central Electricity Generating Board and the Property Services Agency (PSA) Method of Building. Now that profiled metal has become respectable for other uses in a wide range of projects from housing to hospitals, there is a need for information on details and methods of specification related to these types of buildings. The development of new profiles, new methods of curving panels, production of insulated units and methods of installation using horizontal profiles gives greater emphasis to this need.

Sometimes the development of a material within a generally understood technology can leave a gap in the architect's knowledge of this technique. For example, although general principles of curtain walling were explained in Schaal's (1961) excellent design manual, developments in glass production and the introduction of pressure-equalised wall principles have led to new design solutions being considered. Thus designs of rain screen details and suspended glass assemblies, as used at Foster Associates' Willis Faber Dumas headquarters in Ipswich are still not widely understood.

Development of 'High Tech'

Trends in architectural design are now leading young designers and students to explore more and more the use of lightweight construction and clip-in gasket-jointed panels, commonly known as 'High Tech'. The concepts of flexibility and interchangeability, as illustrated by such buildings as Farrell and Grimshaw's Herman Miller factory near Bath (GRP panels), and Foster's Sainsbury Centre (aluminium panels), have now become an acceptable part of an architect's vocabulary. The serviced-shed approach is increasingly familiar, illustrated by the Reliance Controls factory (Team 10), advanced factory units at Kiln Farm (Milton Keynes architects), and factories by the Nicholas Grimshaw Partnership at Warrington and Gillingham. Almost all of these big serviced sheds rely on bright colours, profiled panels and exposed structural grids, all posing new methods of jointing and fixing, not covered by established texts on building construction. Architects' demands for bright colours with contrasting colours for gaskets, window surrounds and flashings have resulted in a need to reconsider the standards of colour matching and finishes of cladding materials.

As new materials and processes are gradually accepted by the architectural profession, manufacturers respond to an increased demand for these new products and materials by introducing their own proprietary solutions on to the market. Under these conditions, the architect needs to exercise his initial assessment of these systems in order to select the component most suitable for his clients' needs. In order to do this he requires a comparative study of the various products to allow him to understand the limitations of the manufacturers' proposals, their performance criteria, finishes and assembly techniques. He needs to be able to distinguish between the various jointing solutions available and analyse the weathering characteristics of each cladding material. This book is intended to meet their requirement.

The main theme underlying the following chapters is the method of production of each of the six cladding types discussed. To understand how a material behaves in use it is first necessary to appreciate the process of its manufacture. Issues such as quality control, cost of production and transportation are fundamental to the proper design of an assembly and affect decisions on size, shape and finish.

A detailed discussion of manufacturing techniques is included in Sebestyen (1977, Ch. VIII) which contains many examples such as forming, casting, rolling, extrusion methods, plate and sheet pressing, sandwich panel fabrication and coating methods, and the reader may wish to refer to this as a basis for some of the discussion in the following chapters.

The performance of a cladding assembly and particularly its watertightness depends upon its method of jointing and, where possible, details are included for each of the applications described. Similarly, the variation in joint size will depend upon the tolerances of construction and the method of fixing used. These are therefore described in detail.

Each chapter contains a description of methods of manufacture, standardisation, performance criteria, finishes, durability, jointing, fixing and methods of transportation, storage and erection. There is no particular reason for the order of the chapters other than perhaps that precast concrete is the most well-known technology, whereas sheet metal and their carrier systems (curtain walling) are the least understood. Glass reinforced polyester and glass fibre reinforced cement tend to be associated with each other, due to the method of their reinforcement, but in fact they are quite different materials, as Chapters 2 and 3 will explain.

Finally, although this book may appear to be about construction, it is also a book about design, for the two are interrelated. It is only through the understanding of technology that the designer can develop his design images with confidence. The following chapters summarise the state of the art of cladding technology and are therefore intended as a contribution towards better design in that field.

References

Architects' Journal (1942) 'Future applications of plastics', *Architects' Journal*, 29. 10. 1942.

Herbert, G. (1978). *Pioneers of Prefabrication – The British Contribution in the Nineteenth Century*, Johns Hopkins University Press: Baltimore and London.

Morris, A. E. J. (1966) *Precast Concrete Cladding*, Fountain Press: London.

Rowe, C. (1956) 'The Chicago frame – Chicago's place in the modern movement'. *Architectural Review*, Nov. 1956, 285–9.

Russell, B. (1981) *Building Systems, Industrialisation and Architecture*, Wiley: London and New York.

Schaal, R. (1961) *Curtain Walls – Design Manual*, Reinhold: New York.

Sebestyen, G. (1977) *Lightweight Building Construction*, George Goodwin: London; Wiley: New York.

Wachsmann, K. (1961) *The Turning Point of Building*, Reinhold: New York.

Wells, H. G. (1902) *Anticipations of the Reaction of Mechanical and Scientific Progress upon Human Life and Thought*. Chapman.

Chapter 1

Precast concrete cladding

Introduction

The three main advantages of using precast as against *in situ* concrete are:

1. Speed of erection.
2. Freedom from shuttering support on-site.
3. Better quality and variety of surface finish because panels are manufactured in controlled factory conditions.

Precast concrete came into its own for use in cladding during the 1950s and early 1960s with the development of high-rise housing. British architects quickly followed the example of Le Corbusier's Marseilles Unité block built between 1947 and 1952. Morris (1966) has described the history of the development of precast concrete in Great Britain, France and the USA up to 1964. One of the most famous examples is the LCC flats at Roehampton Lane (facing slab manufacturer Modular Concrete) which marks the beginning of the continuous use of concrete cladding in the UK.

Precast concrete has been used both for non-loadbearing and for loadbearing cladding units. Both Morris (1966) and the Prestressed Concrete Institute (1973) describe the Police Administration building in Philadelphia, built in 1962, as a major step forward in the structural use of precast concrete wall panels.

Since the collapse of Ronan Point and the consequent introduction of new design rules for all large precast structures in CP110, precast concrete loadbearing cladding has been less popular in the UK. Even so, there have been a number of large projects constructed using non-loadbearing units such as the new Law Courts in Liverpool (architects: Farmer and Dark) now (1981) under construction; the Royal Insurance building in Liverpool, (architects: Tripe and Wakeham Partnership); Kew Public Records Office and the Metal Box Co., at Reading.

A survey carried out by the National Building Agency (1974) showed that only half of the eight large manufacturers of precast concrete units would supply and fix, the remainder preferring to supply only for fixing by a main contractor. Most of the reputable manufacturers will offer a design service and most are members of the British Precast Concrete Federation Ltd.

Design guides

There has now been sufficient experience of the use of precast concrete cladding for a number of design guides to be published on this subject in the last few years, which assist the designer to determine the panel size, shape and composition and to select the surface finish in relationship to the appropriate method of casting the panel. In particular, the PSA Method of Building (1978) gives guidance on such points as:

- panel types and size limitations
- panel web thickness
- design of vertical strengthening ribs
- removal of moisture from behind panels
- open-drained joints
- baffle strips, air seals and flashings
- fixings for panels (cleats and dowels)

Similar issues are discussed in the technical guides by Cement and Concrete Association (1977) and Oram (1978), although these tend to concentrate on current practice in the manufacture of concrete units. Manufacturers also often have their own internal design guides (Scott, 1981).

Useful advice based on American experience is given in the Prestressed Concrete Institute (1973) guide *Architectural Precast Concrete*. Types of finishes related to the method of casting (face-up or face-down) are covered in articles in the *Architects' Journal* by Michael Gage (26.3.69), later developed as a book by the Architectural Press (1974). Gilchrist Wilson's 1963 *Concrete Facing Slabs*, although now rather out of date, gives examples of surface finishes using colour illustrations. R. A. Hartland's (1975) book *Design of Precast Concrete* covers all aspects of precast concrete design, including cladding. Detailing of non-loadbearing precast concrete cladding panels for concrete-framed buildings is also described by Brookes and Yeomans (1981) as part of the *Architects' Journal's* Art of Construction series. Other useful information can be obtained from guides published by British Precast Concrete Federation (1973) and National Building Agency (1967).

Standardisation and adjustable moulds

Economic use of precast concrete can only be achieved if there is a high degree of standardisation in the design of the units. Costs are inevitably higher as greater numbers of panel types are used. There is not only the additional cost of extra moulds, but if moulds have to be continually altered to cast 'specials', the daily casting cycle is disrupted. Moreover, special units require separate stacking and delivery at a particular time. On-site, special lifting and erection procedures may be required for non-standard units. The Cement and Concrete Association (1977) technical report No. 14 gives the main advantages of standardisation as follows:

2

(a) Lower production and erection costs.
(b) Less time for detailing, mould making, and production periods.
(c) Reduced risk of detailing and production errors.
(d) Reduced risk of delays due to units being damaged.
(e) Speedier erection.

The architects should, therefore, make every effort in the early design stages to reduce the number of panel types. Usually it is easier to standardise panel widths than panel heights, due to the frequent requirement to have different storey heights and parapet levels. In this case it is sometimes possible to adjust the design of the supporting *in situ* concrete frame to avoid the use of non-standard panels (see Fig. 1.1). Any additional costs in terms of the shuttering of the

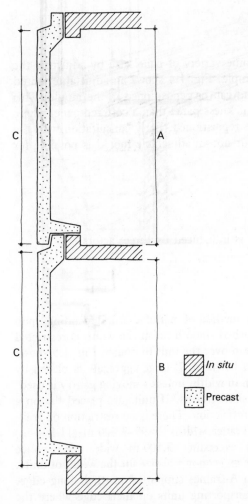

B ▨ *In situ*

▦ Precast

Fig. 1.1 Different frame heights A and B allowing use of standard panel heights C.

3

main structure can be offset against the savings in greater standardisation of precast units. Part of the skill of designing with precast units is this choice between standardising precast and *in situ* construction. A good example is illustrated by the student residence for Christ's College, Cambridge (architect: Denys Lasdun and Partners), where the architects have used a basically precast aesthetic *in situ* construction using a limited range of panel forms (see Fig. 1.2).

If it is not possible to adjust the structure then the design should be such that the number of moulds required are kept to a minimum. For example, one way in which a limited range of panels can be used to produce an interesting elevation pattern is illustrated by the façade of a small infill scheme at 428, Singel, Amsterdam (architect: Abel Cahen), where four spandrel panels, simple in shape, are used in an innovative way to give an interesting elevation, while still using the same panel profile (Fig. 1.3).

Adjustable moulds

It may also be possible to provide some variety of panel size by adjusting the mould during manufacture. For example, Fig. 1.4 shows an adjustable mould for face-up casting where the stop end can be repositioned in the mould. This is more easily done with a uniform thickness panel than a coffered panel where the coffer former will also need to be repositioned. Early consultation with the manufacturer will establish whether or not an adjustable mould is possible for any particular project.

Size of panels

The size of the precast concrete unit is influenced by three factors:

1. Ease of manufacture.
1. Method of transportation.
3. Weight of unit for lifting.

The width of the unit is related to the method of manufacture, depending upon the type of finish required. For a polished smooth finish the width is restricted to about 1.200 m to allow a man to lean over the unit to polish. Fig. 1.5 shows a typical width of unit being polished by hand. If large aggregate is placed by hand then units should not exceed 2 m in width, unless a moving gantry is used.

Transportation will also limit the size of units. If units are placed flat on a trailer the width is related to payload restriction. There is no restriction on trailers up to 2.895 m (9 ft 6 in) wide. Trailer widths 2.895–3.500 m (11 ft 6 in) need police permission, and loads exceeding 3.500 m wide need police escort. Thus 1.200–3.00 m seems to be an economical size for the width of units.

Wider units can be transported on A-frames supported on their long edge. Figure 1.6 shows two methods of transporting units on their edge where the maximum height when loaded should not exceed 4.880 m. Allowing for the

Fig. 1.2 Students' residences for Christ's College, Cambridge (architect: Denys Lasdun & Partners) (courtesy of D. King).

Fig. 1.3 Apartment infill block in Amsterdam (architect: Abel Cahen) (courtesy of Pat Sheldon).

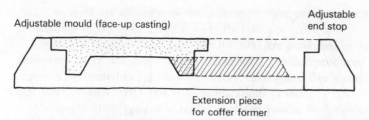

Fig. 1.4   Adjustable mould for a variety of panel sizes.

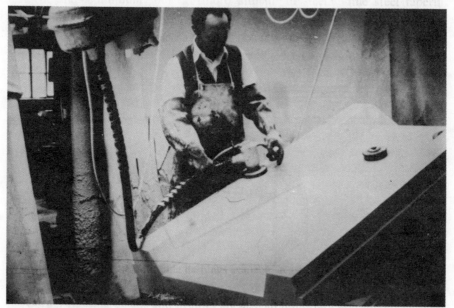

Fig. 1.5   Cladding unit in course of finishing (courtesy of Empire Stone Company Ltd).

height of the trailer and bearers, panels of up to 4.130 m width are possible. Fig. 1.7 shows wall panels being loaded on an A-framed trailer.

Lengths of units are normally 3 × width and will also be affected by the maximum lengths of the trailers, normally not longer than 12 m. Thickness of the panel is related to the required cover for the reinforcement in the panel web (see Fig. 1.17 panel web thickness). As a rough guide to decide typical thickness of panel related to the longest side of the unit the following table can be used.

Panel length (m)	Approx. thickness (mm)
1.0	65
2.0	75
3.0	90
4.0	100
5.5	125

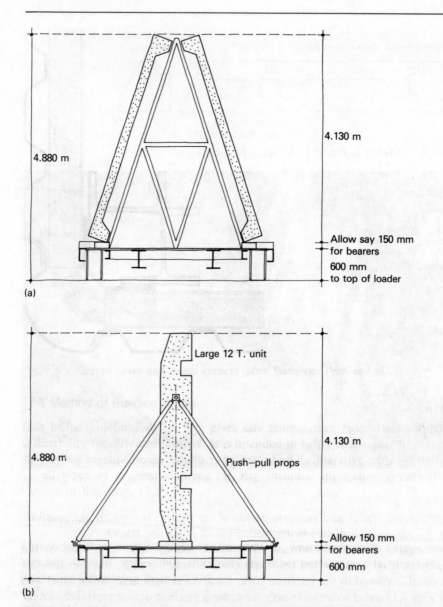

(a)

4.880 m

4.130 m

Allow say 150 mm
for bearers

600 mm
to top of loader

(b)

4.880 m

4.130 m

Large 12 T. unit

Push–pull props

Allow 150 mm
for bearers

600 mm

Fig. 1.6 Width of panel related to safe height during transportation: (a) units transported on A-frames supported on edge; (b) large unit held vertically.

Once the panel width, length and thickness have been determined, the cubic volume × density of concrete will determine the overall weight of the unit.

In most cases wall panels should not exceed 7 t to allow easy handling during manufacture and on-site. However, some manufacturers have facilities for handling units up to 20 t in weight.

Fig. 1.7 Window units being loaded on to 'A'-frame trailer (courtesy of Empire Stone Company Ltd).

Types of moulds

The choice of material for the moulds is usually determined by the number of uses and is essentially a matter of economics. Thus, although moulds may be made of timber, steel or GRP, there is a considerable cost difference between these materials. Another factor influencing the choice of mould material may be the time taken to make the mould and the rate of output required to meet the erection programme. Shape and size of the units to be cast may also be a consideration.

Timber moulds are normally used because of their versatility in manufacture. They are certainly the cheapest method for simple panel shapes, with an average of 20–30 castings possible for a complicated panel, and 50–60 castings from each mould for a more simple shape. However, they suffer from wear more than steel moulds and do not have the same degree of accuracy. Panels are normally manufactured to BS CP297, with a manufacturing variability of ± 3 mm. Inaccuracies in bow can be a problem with long units using timber moulds, but these can be reduced by the use of push/pull props (see Fig. 1.8). A high standard

9

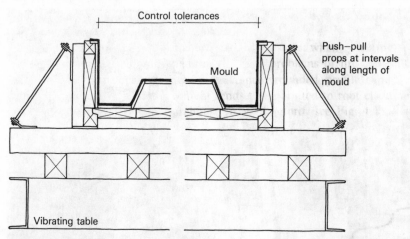

Fig. 1.8 Push–pull props to reduce bowing of timber moulds (as used by Empire Stone Company Ltd).

of finish can be obtained on the moulding by spraying the mould surface with a thin film of GRP.

Steel moulds offer a better degree of accuracy of manufacture. Also more panels, at least 150 castings, can be made from the same mould. However, their cost is greater than that of timber and they take longer to make. Steel moulds are usually only used for long runs of absolutely standard units, as they are less easily adjusted than timber moulds.

Glass reinforced polyester moulds, although offering a better standard of accuracy, are more easily damaged and may need frequent repair. Thus, the life of the mould is longer than timber, but shorter than steel. When deeply coffered panels are required, GRP may be cheaper than timber and also copies of the mould can be made more easily. It will, of course, be necessary to make the master mould in timber or fibrous plaster to cast the GRP moulds. They are usually used for any unusually shaped or deeply coffered panels. A thin skin of GRP can be used in a timber mould for a better standard of finish (see above).

Casting method

The choice of casting method is normally related to the type of finish required and to the mould table available to the supplier. Three alternative casting methods are normally available for factory production (see Fig. 1.9):

1. Face-up casting.
2. Face-down casting.
3. Tilting moulds.

Face-up casting allows various surface finishes to be applied to the top surface while the units is still in the mould. It is not suitable for mosaic or tiled finishes or where a smooth surface is required. A disadvantage is that the 'fat' tends to

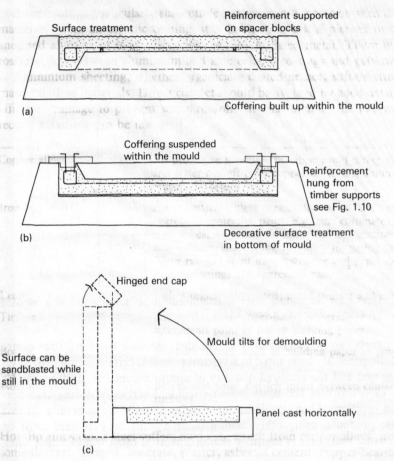

Fig. 1.9 Three alternative methods of casting: (a) face-up: (b) face-down; (c) tilting moulds.

rise to the surface of the concrete, resulting in a weaker face. However, the reinforcement may be easily supported on spacer blocks without detracting from the external appearance.

Face-down casting is most suitable for mosaic, tiled and profiled surfaces. However, if the latter require a surface treatment, this cannot begin until the panel is demoulded and production will consequently be slower. Support of the reinforcement to ensure adequate cover needs attention. Figure 1.10 shows a typical device used by Empire Stone Ltd, to control the cover to the reinforcement. Lifting sockets or loops in the back of the panel are easily inserted for demoulding. If these are used, care should be taken to ensure either that they do not interfere with the erection of the panel, or that they are cut off before delivery to site.

Tilting moulds are ideally suited to casting panels of uniform profiles. Not all

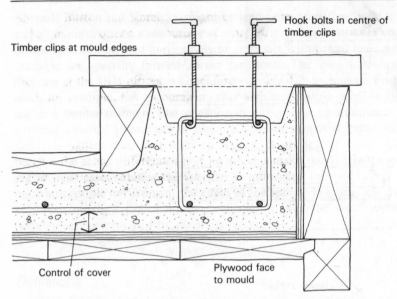

Fig. 1.10 Device for controlling cover to reinforcement in face-down casting (as used by Empire Stone Company Ltd).

coffered panels can be satisfactorily demoulded. Because handling stresses are less after the panel has been tilted to a vertical position, certain lifting provisions can be omitted and the required quantity of reinforcement for handling can be reduced, in which case the units must be handled vertically during transportation and erection. Thus panels made in tilting moulds are generally thinner than those produced using other casting methods. In this case care must be taken to ensure that there is adequate reinforcement to resist wind loading when fixed in place.

A summary of the characteristics of alternative casting methods is given in Appendix 1 of PSA Method of Building (1978). In addition to these factory production methods, site casting using vertical concrete shutters has been developed by the Building Research Establishment (BRE) and is known as 'battery' casting.

Tolerances

Three kinds of inaccuracy arise in building: those of manufacture, those of setting out the *in situ* construction, and those of erection of the precast components. British Standard CP297: 1972 *Precast concrete cladding (non-loadbearing)* gives the permissible deviations of manufacturing inaccuracy as + 0 − basis. British Standard CP116 Part II: 1969 *Structural use of precast concrete* gives deviations on ± basis. Manufacturers prefer to work with deviations ± from the worksize, and common practice allows for deviations of ± 1.5 mm and ± 6 mm depending on panel sizes up to 6 m in length and height. When used in conjunction with *in situ* concrete frame construction with typical deviations of ± 15 mm or more, then joints of 5–25 mm between panels can be expected.

In addition to these 'induced' deviations, 'inherent' movement deviations can also be expected, caused by shrinkage, elastic deformation, creep or changes in thermal and moisture content. A variety of factors influence the extent of these movements and, although not susceptible to precise calculation, generally they are in the order of 1 mm per 3 m depending upon the range of temperature expected. These movements are, of course, reversible and should be allowed for in the design of fixings.

Handling of units during transportation and on-site

Panels require to be lifted from the mould and handled through storage, transportation and finally erection on-site. Lifting provision is required in the panels at each stage. One of the main points to consider in the design of precast concrete panels is their weight for handling. Most manufacturers would recommend panels not exceeding 7 t for lifting and 'shuffling' into place on-site. This can often place a restriction on the size of the panel, depending upon the density of the concrete used, and architects must, therefore, be aware of any weight restriction when determining panel size.

Lifting provision for transportation and erection should, if possible, be above the centre of gravity, so that when the panel is suspended it will hang in a vertical plane. Tilting of the panels during lifting on-site can cause difficulties in placing and fixing. Often it is not possible to suspend a highly profiled panel, such as a spandrel panel, from its outer face, due to difficulties of patching over the fixing sockets. Special lifting devices are then used (see Fig. 1.11) to support

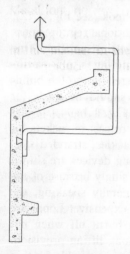

Fig. 1.11 Special lifting tackle for profiled units.

Fig. 1.12 Special lifting device for cranked units (courtesy of Empire Stone Company Ltd).

the panel and keep the centre of gravity below the crane hook (see Fig. 1.12).

Panels are often transported horizontally and require additional reinforcement and lifting provision for handling when lifted into their vertical position. One method of reducing the stress on the panel during such handling is to use a tilting platform (see Fig. 1.13). Tight access for crane jibs in relation to the building form should be checked in advance and allowance should be made for clearance for the jib of the crane above panel fixings (see Fig. 1.14).

Fixings for handling are usually loops of reinforcement or cast-in sockets for use with patent lifting devices which take the form of shackles, stranded steel loops, collared eyes or clip-on bolts. Common patent lifting devices are shown in Fig. 1.15. Screw-in lifting devices should not be used singly because of the danger of them becoming unscrewed during lifting. Generally speaking, the shackle device has been found to be the most reliable but expensive. Loops are the most common method. These can be left intact or burnt off when not required. Collared eyes and shackle are useful for side-hung lifting provision. Clip-on fixings are useful, but the width of hold makes them unsuitable for thin slabs.

Fig. 1.13   Tilting platform as used at Liverpool Royal Insurance building (courtesy of Herbert Penn).

Levelling devices

Levelling devices can be used to facilitate panel assembly. They take the form of a cast-in threaded plate and a bolt which engages in the plate and bears on the floor slab.

Shape of precast concrete cladding panels

The principal types of non-loadbearing panel are storey height and spandrel units (see Fig. 1.16). These are either of uniform thickness or coffered at their edge to provide a jointing profile. Most panels employ strengthening 'ribs' as beams to transfer dead and vertically applied loads to the structure, the panel 'web' then acting as a slab spanning between these beams.

The shape of precast concrete cladding units is therefore related to:

- panel web thickness
- horizontal support/restraint nibs
- vertical strengthening ribs

Panel web thickness

Although CP297 indicates maximum rib spacing and minimum web thickness for coffered panels, in practice the web thickness is governed by the requirements

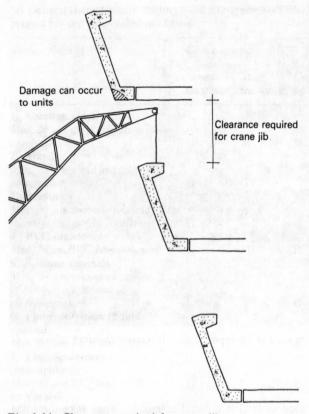

Damage can occur to units

Clearance required for crane jib

Fig. 1.14 Clearance required for crane jib.

of cover to the reinforcement. This is dependent on the degree of exposure to weather (which CP110 Part I: 1972, p. 54 lists as mild, moderate, severe and very severe), the grade of concrete used (25 N, 30 N/mm²) and whether a facing mix is required to obtain a special finish. Figure 1.17 shows the depths to be allowed for panel web thickness for two types of concrete mixes. The thickness of the panel web is determined from the following factors:

• the external cover to reinforcement
• the zone of reinforcement
• the internal cover to reinforcement

The depth of external and internal cover should be determined according to the grade of concrete to be used and the conditions of exposure. Normally, external cover is either 40 or 50 mm and internal cover 20 or 25 mm. A zone of 25 mm should be allowed for the reinforcement, stiffening bars and variability of placing the steel in the mould. For most conditions a nominal thickness of 100 mm can be used for web thickness in design. Using a span: depth ratio of 27 the web would then span 2.7 m.

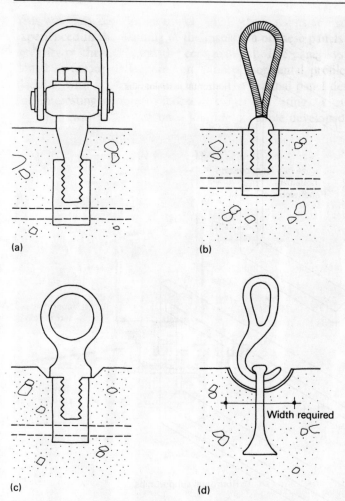

Fig. 1.15 Principal lifting devices: (a) shackle; (b) Loop; (c) collared eye; (d) clip-on.

Horizontal support and restraint nibs

The depth of the horizontal support nib is determined from the loadbearing and fixing requirements. The most important consideration is that there should be a minimum bearing of 100 mm on the structural slab plus an allowance of 25 mm for any inaccuracies in the edge of the slab and any danger of spalling. Figure 1.18 shows the minimum dimensions of the horizontal support nib and its bearing depending upon the type of fixings to be used. Allow for 175 mm with dowel fixings and 125 mm using cleat fixings.

In addition to providing space for reinforcement, the height of the nib is usually affected by the type of fixing used and whether or not it is necessary to provide cast-in fixing sockets. Where an angle cleat fixing is used the suggested height of nibs is 150 mm. For a dowel fixing this can be reduced to 125 mm.

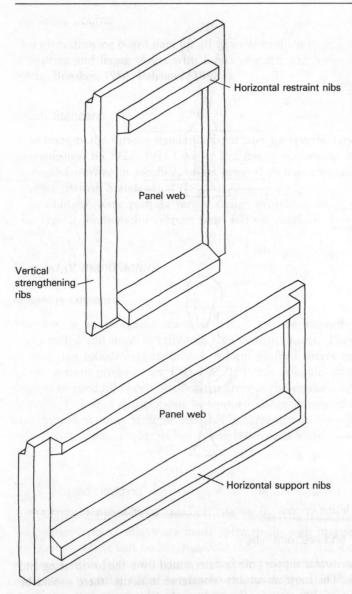

Horizontal restraint nibs

Panel web

Vertical
strengthening
ribs

Panel web

Horizontal support nibs

Fig. 1.16 Strengthening ribs and support nibs.

Vertical strengthening ribs

The depth of the vertical strengthening ribs is related to the span between the supports and should be determined from CP110. For coffered panels the web is designed using a span: depth ratio of 1 : 27, whereas the ribs can be designed as beams with a span: depth ratio of 1 : 17. Sufficient depth is often necessary to accommodate the elements of an open-drained joint (see Figs. 1.19 and 1.25),

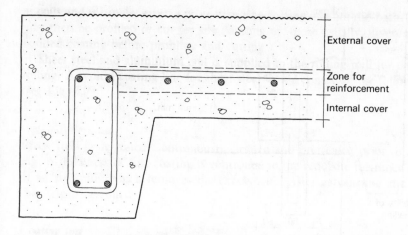

	Concrete grade	
	25 N/m²	30 N/m²
External cover	50	40
Reinforcement zone	25	25
Internal cover	25	20
Total depth	100	85

Fig. 1.17 Panel web thickness related to zone for reinforcement and cover.

especially where the profile incorporates a drainage groove or where an upstand is provided at the head of the panel. Figure 1.19 shows vertical strengthening ribs of 250 mm to coincide with the depth of a panel needed to incorporate an upstand joint.

The breadth of the rib is governed by such factors as:

• cover to vertical reinforcement
• the dimensions of columns at panel junctions
• the accommodation of push/pull sockets for alignment and fixing

Additional cover will be required if open-drained joint grooves are incorporated in the edge of the panel.

Figure 1.20 shows that for panels abutting columns a breadth of 100–125 mm is normally sufficient, but when the panels occur in front of the structural columns this may have to be increased to allow for the dimension of the column, so that panel fixing can be within the rib dimension.

Jointing

Sealants

Sealant joints are designed to provide a complete watertight barrier in the form of a single-stage joint positioned towards the panel face. The main types of seal-

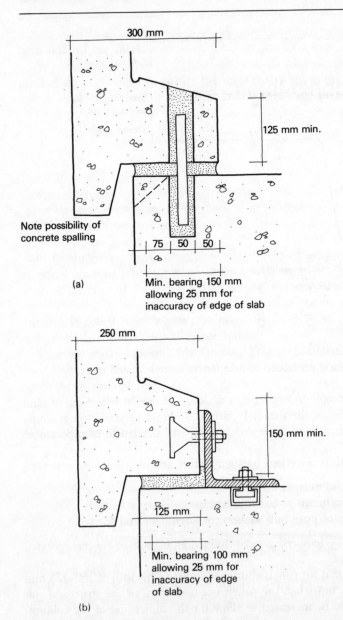

Fig. 1.18 Minimum dimensions of horizontal support nibs: (a) dowel fixing; (b) cleat fixing.

ant joints for use with concrete cladding are polysulphide (one and two-part) and acrylic. Sealant joints are often used for highly profiled units such as spandrel or parapet panels.

Two-part polysulphide sealants are most commonly used because they have

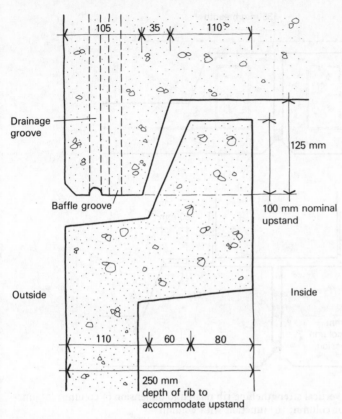

Fig. 1.19 Depth of rib to accommodate upstand at head of panel.

better movement capability and thus can offer greater joint size ranges. On the other hand, on large jobs with several mixes the colour of sealant can vary, and some manufacturers prefer to use one-part polysulphide with which the colour is more constant.

Rectangular or circular-section sealant backing strips of closed cell polyethylene foam are used to ensure the correct depth of sealant and to separate it from incompatible materials which could cause its breakdown (see Fig. 1.21).

It must be accepted that sealant joints will need to be repointed during the life of the building, as the proven life of the best sealants is as yet only twenty years. However, sealants in locations protected from the effects of ultraviolet light and extremes of weather may have a greater life expectancy than those in more exposed positions.

Some cladding manufacturers consider that sealant joints are only suitable in conditions of mild or moderate site exposure and look to gasket joints as offering a more stable jointing product, particularly when used as a two-stage joint in conjunction with an air seal.

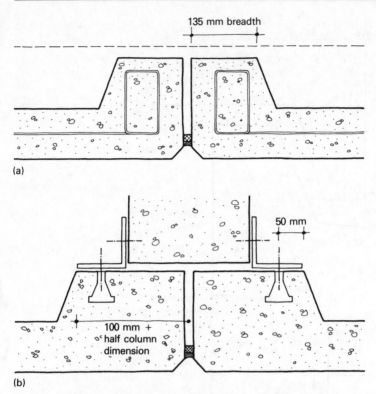

Fig. 1.20 Breadth of vertical strengthening rib related to dimension of column: (a) junction without column; (b) junction with column.

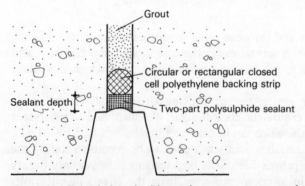

Fig. 1.21 Polyethylene backing strip to ensure correct depth of sealant.

Open-drained joints

Most popular of such gasket joints is the open-drained baffle joint. This joint, first introduced from Scandinavia in the 1950s, is now in widespread use and with proper detailing, correct specification and control of installation on-site, it has proved to be fairly successful. Correct detailing, however, is essential. Open-drained joints are explained in the BRE Digest No. 85: 1967 *Joints between concrete wall panels: open-drained joints* (1967). This covers principles and recommendations on details, especially flashings at cross-over joints (see Fig. 1.22).

The principle of the open-drained joint is to use the geometry of the joint to trap the majority of the rain in an outer zone and to provide a barrier (air seal) at the back of the joint to avoid air and water (which gets past the baffle) penetrating into the building. Although the baffle strip acts as a primary barrier

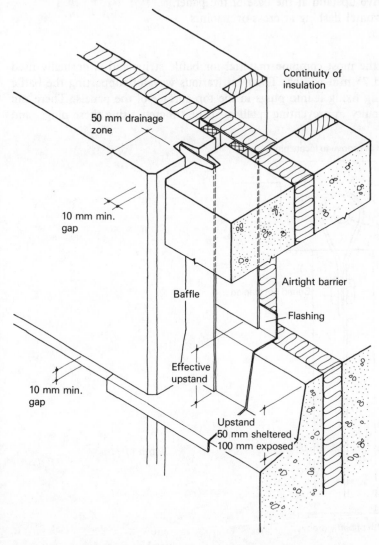

Continuity of insulation

50 mm drainage zone

10 mm min. gap

Airtight barrier

Baffle

Flashing

Effective upstand

10 mm min. gap

Upstand
50 mm sheltered
100 mm exposed

Fig. 1.22 Cross-over open-drained joint (after BRE Digest No. 85).

to wind-driven rain, the real effectiveness of the joint depends on maintaining the performance of the air seal. The theory is that being positioned at the back of the joint the seal is sheltered by the baffle from the ultraviolet light and direct rain and is subject to less thermal and moisture movement than if it were positioned nearer the face of the panel.

The main elements of the open-drained joint are therefore:

(a) The baffle strip.
(b) The baffle groove.
(c) The air seal.
(d) An effective upstand at the base of the panel.
(e) The horizontal flashing at cross-over joints.

Baffle strips

Neoprene is the most common material for baffle strips and is normally used in 50, 63 and 75 mm widths. There are various ways of supporting the baffle strip, including fixing it into plugs in the top surface of the panels. There can be some difficulty in preventing spalling of the concrete using these plugs, and

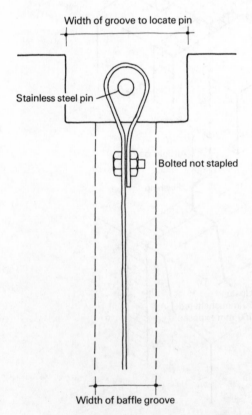

Fig. 1.23 Method of restraining the baffle using a stainless steel pin.

another method devised to facilitate renewal of the baffle is to turn it over a stainless steel pin restrained by bolting through the return ends. The baffle should not be fixed over the pin using staples alone (see Fig. 1.23). The steel pin is located in grooves on either side of the panel joint which should be wide enough to contain the diameter of the pin (not less than 6 mm) plus two thicknesses of baffle. This will probably be wider than the baffle groove in the side of the panel.

When using baffle strips these should not be stretched before cutting at the base of the panel, otherwise they spring back up the joints and are then too short.

Baffle grooves
Grooves are normally formed by fixing a timber insert to the edge of the mould and a width of 15–25 mm is normally sufficient to allow a screw fixing and demoulding from the mould. The depth of the groove will vary according to the joint range expected, but 35 mm is normally adequate to accommodate a 75 mm baffle.

The recommended distance of the baffle groove from the front of the panel

Fig. 1.24 Baffle fixed over stainless steel pin for easy renewal.

is 50 mm, which should be increased to 75 mm if an additional drainage groove is provided (see Fig. 1.25).

Air seals

Air seals can be in the form of flexible membranes, gaskets, compressible foam strips and sealants. In practice this seal has proved difficult to apply. The main difficulty is that of providing a satisfactory air seal at the back of the joint, especially in positions where panels pass in front of floor slabs or where panel joints occur on the centre line of concrete columns. In this case it is not normally possible to apply the seal directly to the back face of the joint.

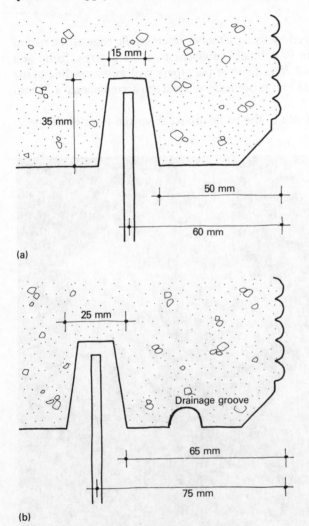

(a)

(b)

Fig. 1.25 Depth of baffle groove from the face of the panel: (a) without drainage groove; (b) with drainage groove.

Upstands

The matching upstand and downstand profile at the horizontal joint is one of the primary features of the open-drained system. The height of the upstand and downstand is related to the site exposure conditions, as defined in BRE Digest 127 (*An index of exposure to driving rain*). The effective lap and the width of the horizontal joint are added to determine the actual height of the upstand or downstand (see Fig. 1.26). For sheltered conditions the effective lap should be 50 mm and for severe conditions this should be increased to 100 mm.

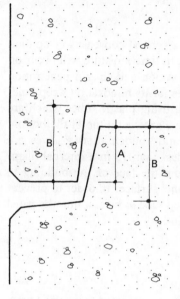

Site exposure	A	B
Sheltered	50	75
Moderate	75	100
Severe	100	125

Fig. 1.26 Heights of upstands and downstands. A = effective lap, B = actual lap or downstand.

Flashings

A horizontal flashing must be provided at the junction of horizontal and vertical joints. The principal materials used for flashings are bitumen/polythene or butyl rubber. The width of the flashing should be 300 mm in order to span the vertical joint.

Gasket joints

Although a number of gasket joints have been used, including cellular, tubular, cruciform and fir-cone gaskets, they all require to be constantly under compression with continuous contact with the panel edge. This is not easy to achieve, due to the variation of joint widths normally attainable on-site (typically 10–30 mm). The possibility of blow-holes and other unevenness on the concrete panel joint profile also make continuous contact with the panel edge difficult to attain. Cruciform gaskets are produced in rolls and are difficult to straighten out.

The cost of the jointing system depends on the quality of the materials used. For sealant joints the cost is generally related to the volume of sealant and is influenced by the expected range of joint sizes. For gaskets, the labour in cutting and welding of sections and correct selection of gasket size is of particular significance.

Removal of moisture from behind panels

No matter which type of joint is used, there is a general consensus of opinion by BRE and panel manufacturers that from time to time moisture will occur on the inner surface of panels as a result of condensation and/or rain penetration and panels should be designed to include facilities for its removal by weep holes in the panel. These are produced during casting using plastic tubes which are left in the moulding. Condensation is collected in a groove on top of the bottom horizontal ribs. Different weep tube designs and condensation grooves are shown in Fig. 1.27. Weep tubes should not be less than 13 mm internal diameter to prevent blocking and should project from the face of the building to prevent, as far as possible, any staining of the panel surface. In order to prevent such staining, it is sometimes possible for the weep tube to be cast into the panel so that it drains moisture into the horizontal joint.

Panel fixings

Panels can be either top-hung from the structure or supported from their base. Nibs projecting from the back of the panel transmit the load to the structure by means of a mortar bed. Panels can then be restrained by either dowel bars or angle cleats, both of which must be fixed so as to permit vertical movements arising from the deformation of the structure or movement of the panels. Various combinations of dowel and cleat fixings are shown in Fig. 1.28. Contractors often prefer cleat fixings at the top with dowel or cleat fixings at the bottom (types a and b) because this facilitates quick erection; however, building inspectors sometimes prefer type (c), overhanging the slab, as in theory should the fixing fail the panel would fall inwards under their own weight and wind loading.

Although the dimensional inaccuracies in manufacture of medium-sized precast concrete panels is not likely to be in excess of ± 3 mm, the inaccuracies imposed during assembly, due to deviations in the frame and erection deviations on the panels, are likely to be much more than this, possibly ± 25 mm. Thus tolerance must be allowed in the method of fixing and in the allowable clearance between the panels and the structure, to take account of such inaccuracies of construction. Allowance must be made in the design of the fixings for thermal

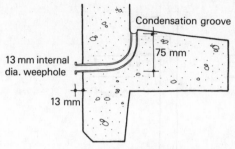

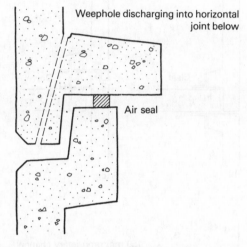

Fig. 1.27 Alternative positions of weepholes.

movement of the panel. Avoid three fixings at different levels (see Fig. 1.29). Two types of fixing are in common use in addition to the fixings for handling listed earlier. These are:

- angle cleats
- dowels

Angle cleats

Although usually used for top restraint of panels, angle cleats may also be employed at the base support position. There should be at least two cleats per panel, irrespective of panel size, and their size should be calculated by a structural engineer according to the loading for each job. They should be designed to give three-dimensional adjustments by the use of slotted holes and/or by packing pieces. Figure 1.28 shows a typical angle cleat bracket system with packing allowance adjustment at right angles to the face of the building. Vertical adjust-

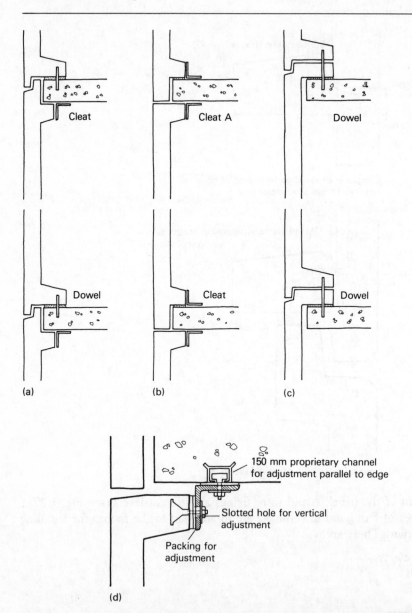

Fig. 1.28 Various combinations of dowel and cleat fixings: (a) cleat top dowel bottom; (b) cleats top and bottom; (c) dowels top and bottom; (d) detail at A.

ment is provided by the use of a slotted hole and low friction washer, and horizontal adjustment is provided by means of a 150 mm length of proprietary channel cast into the floor slab. Care is needed in the accurate location of such channels during the casting of the slab and reliable placing is more easily achieved when this channel is cast into soffit of the slab (where it can be fastened

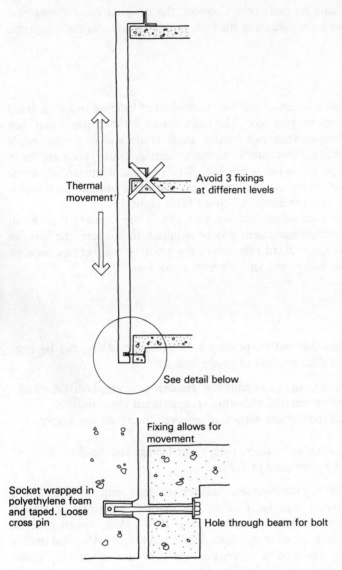

Thermal movement

Avoid 3 fixings at different levels

See detail below

Fixing allows for movement

Socket wrapped in polyethylene foam and taped. Loose cross pin

Hole through beam for bolt

Fig. 1.29 Allowance in the design of fixings for thermal movement and inaccuracy.

to the shuttering), rather than in the top surface.

Bolts fixing the angle cleats are normally fixed to cast-in sockets or expanding sleeves. Cast-in sockets are used with precast concrete, as they can be accurately cast in place in the factory. However, with *in situ* concrete, their precise location cannot be guaranteed and channels are used to allow adjustment. Where channels are not suitable the structure is drilled to receive bolts with expanding sleeves, taking care to avoid the reinforcement.

In all fixings relying on bolts or set screws, the designer must ensure that there is adequate space for tightening the bolt, or other device, in the completed assembly.

Dowel fixings

Dowel bar fixings are a common and simple method of locating and restraining the panel at its bottom support nibs. The main reason for their use is that they are considerably cheaper than non-ferrous angle cleats and can more easily accommodate dimensional inaccuracies in the structure. Usually they are set in a 50 mm × 50 mm pocket in the *in situ* floor slab, a 50 mm diameter hole being provided in the panel to receive the dowel bar. The space around the dowel is grouted with either neat cement or an epoxy resin grout.

Where dowels are used in conjunction with panels supported at their head, some provision for vertical movement may be required. In this case, the bars can be bound with Sellotape to avoid adhesion of the grout. A resilient pad between the panel nibs allows movement and prevents grout loss.

Finishes

The range of finishes that can be produced on precast cladding can be summarised according to their method of production as:

1. Surfaces cast direct from the mould, e.g. smooth concrete, board marked concrete, grooved or serrated including reconstructed stone finishes.
2. Finishes in which the cement surface is removed to expose the aggregate in the concrete.
3. Applied finishes, such as mosaics, tiles, stone facings and bricks.
4. Surfaces textured by tamping or shaping.

The various methods to produce these finishes are dealt with by Gage (1974) in his guide to exposed concrete finishes. In addition, examples of various exposed aggregate finishes can be seen in Oram (1978). Most precast concrete cladding panels use such exposed aggregate finishes and their colour and texture is largely effected by the type of aggregate used. The use of applied finishes affects the type of casting used. (See Fig. 1.9.)

Weathering

The quantity of rain-water, the velocity and the angle at which it hits a building, change for different positions in the building and therefore one must expect unequal weathering of the parts. This is particularly true for precast concrete where the water absorption can cause blotches or streaking on finished surfaces. Concrete finishes vary considerably in their ability to take up and release dirt

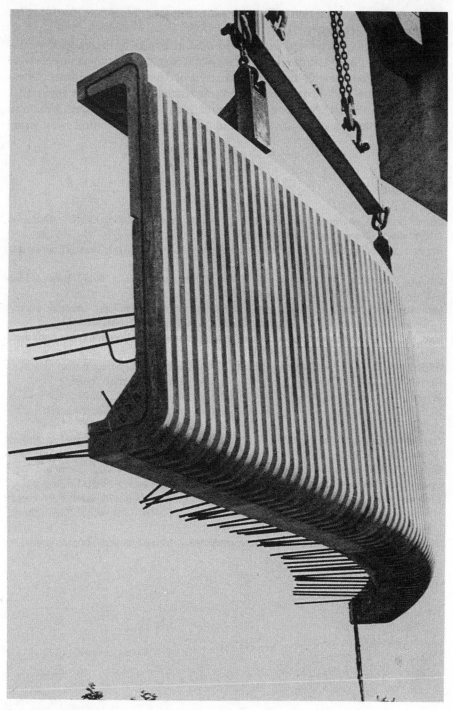

Fig. 1.30 Ribbed concrete panels (courtesy of D. King).

under weathering conditions. They should, therefore, be chosen for so called 'self-cleansing' properties.

Some buildings have been designed to take advantage of the unequal weathering in the profile of the panel; for example, faceted panels (now removed) were used at the Mathematics building at Liverpool University (architects: Westwood, Piet, Pool and Smart). Vertical ribs or striations also help the appearance of panels. Panels for Portsmouth Dockyard (Arup Associates) were produced by Minsterstone, using concrete moulds and ribbed to control weathering marks.

References

British Precast Concrete Federation (1973) *Precast Concrete Cladding Panels – Method of Attachment, Support and Joint Design,*

Brookes, A. and Yeomans, D. (1981) *Precast Concrete Cladding (Art of Construction Series),* Architects' *Journal,* 24.6.1981.

Building Research Establishment (1967) *Joints between Concrete Wall Panels: Open-drained Joints,* BRE Digest 85, Aug. 1967.

Cement & Concrete Association *Guide to Precast Concrete Cladding,* Concrete Society Technical Report No. 14. Concrete Society: London, (1970). May 1977.

Gage, M. (1974) *Finishes in Precast Concrete,* Architectural Press: London. (Also published in *Architects' Journal,* 26.3.1969).

Gilchrist Wilson, J. (1963) *Concrete Facing Slabs,* Cement & Concrete Assoc.: London.

Hartland, R. A. (1975) *Design of Precast Concrete,* Surrey University Press.

Morris, A. E. J. (1966) *Precast Concrete Cladding,* Fountain Press: London.

National Building Agency (1967) *Drained Joints in Precast Concrete Cladding,* NBA, Oct. 1967.

National Building Agency (1974) *Precast Concrete Cladding* (Report No. 467), Project No. 1041.01. NBA, Dec. 1974.

Oram, J. (1978) *Precast Concrete Cladding,* Cement & Concrete Assoc.: London.

Prestressed Concrete Institute (1973) *Architectural Precast Concrete,* PCI: Chicago.

Property Services Agency Method of Building (1978) *Technical Guidance on Precast Concrete – Non-loadbearing Cladding,* MOB doc. 01.704 (2nd edn). PSA Library: London, Dec. 1978.

Scott, T. (1981) 'Precast concrete panel construction', Internal paper – Empire Stone Co. Ltd: Narborough, Leicester.

Chapter 2

Glass reinforced polyester

Introduction

Many different materials have been used to form composites within the field of reinforced plastics. The concept is to combine a strong tensile fibrous material, to give tensile strength, with a resinous binder to hold the material together and provide compressive strength. Thus GRP is a composite of durable resin with glass fibre reinforcement. Its principal characteristics are:

1. It has a high strength and low density leading to lightweight products. Despite its high tensile strength, however, it has a low modulus of elasticity and, therefore, high loads can only be sustained at the expense of large deflections.
2. Glass reinforced polyester has good corrosion and weather resistance, making it suitable for long-term use in external conditions.
3. Its most useful characteristic is that, being a thermosetting material, it can be moulded without the use of pressure or high temperature. This characteristic makes the moulding of relatively short runs of large awkward shapes possible. It also gives GRP its versatility of appearance as, in theory, almost any colour or texture can be produced.

Glass reinforced polyester is more expensive on a volume basis than most other building materials, and its use in thin sections, therefore, to achieve cost comparability is essential.

To understand how GRP behaves in use, it is first necessary to appreciate the process of manufacture. The 'gel coat', a layer of resin which forms the outer surface of the GRP, provides protection for a mixture of glass fibre reinforcement and a polyester 'lay-up' resin. Coloured pigments can be added either to the resin – or to the gel coat – and, in addition, chemicals and fillers can be added to improve the fire retardancy of the composite.

The liquid resin is 'polymerised' or cured into a hard solid by the addition of chemical catalysts which are mixed into the resin shortly before the material is laid up – in the mould – with the glass fibre. Any of these factors can change for a particular application. Unlike profiled steel, aluminium or even precast concrete where, within limits, the constituents remain constant, with GRP there are a number of variables which could affect the long-term durability of the material – unless designed with care. In most cases the laminate is laid up using hand rollers or spray techniques in contact moulds. Mechanical processes such as vacuum bags or press mouldings are only really applicable for long production runs.

GRP production

Thus the factors of GRP production to be discussed further are:
(a) The polyester resin.
(b) The glass fibre reinforcement.
(c) Fabrication – the mould.
(d) Quality control and faults in curing.

Polyester resin

The resin is supplied as a viscous syrup which, when chemically activated, sets to a hard solid, binding the glass fibre together. Pigments can be added to the resin to provide the required colour. Finely ground filler may also be added to increase the resin viscosity or improve its fire performance. Ultraviolet stabilisers may be added to reduce discoloration of GRP when exposed to sunlight. These pigments, fillers and stabilisers, however, in turn may affect the properties of the resin. The liquid polyester resin is polymerised into its hard solid state by the addition of chemical catalysts, preferably under controlled heat conditions. (Polyester materials are thermosetting, which signifies that they cannot be turned back into liquid form, unlike thermoplastic materials, such as polyethylene.) The mixing of resin and catalyst takes place shortly before the material is required for fabrication. The hardening process is sometimes called 'curing' and the rate of cure is temperature dependent.

A vital part played in the manufacturing process is that of ensuring the final product is fully cured, for it is only in this state that structural and dimensional stability is assured. Excessive catalyst will cause the mixture to overheat since the chemical reaction produced is exothermic resulting in cracking and crazing, while inadequate catalyst will produce an inadequate state of curing. (Such typical faults are contained in Ch. 6 of Scott Bader Ltd, (1980); see Fig. 2.1.) Usually, after demoulding, the panels are placed in a curing box under controlled temperature and humidity conditions. The manufacturer can make special curing boxes for large panels, although space in the factory may not necessarily be available and the optimum size of the kilns available should be checked in advance of the design.

Glass fibre reinforcement

Molten glass can be drawn out into a filament of glass fibre and in this form has an ultimate tensile strength per area of ten times that of steel. The existence of

(a)

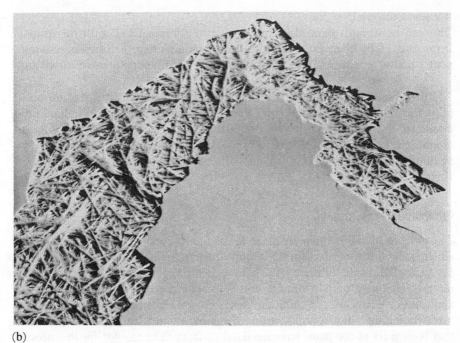

(b)

Fig. 2.1　Faults: (a) crazing of GRP surface; (b) internal dry patch (both courtesy of Scott Bader Co. Ltd, 1980).

the material has been known since the Egyptian XVIIIth Dynasty, about 1500 BC (Fibreglass Ltd, 1977a). However, glass fibres of sufficient fineness and consistency for reinforced plastics were not commercially available until the 1930s.

Although several types of glass can be drawn into fibres, the standard fibre used for all resin systems is E Glass, which is a high-quality electrical grade glass fibre. This is bundled together to form strands which in turn can be processed into various products.

Chopped strand mat
This is the most common form of general purpose reinforcement which is used, mainly for the hand laminating process.

Continuous strand mat
This is where the strands are not chopped, but just allowed to swirl randomly. The product is used for press moulding and resin injection moulding.

Continuous rovings
These consist of long bundles of fibres which are fed into a machine which chops and sprays them on to the moulding in conjunction with the resin. This 'spray-up' technique is used very widely to reduce the labour content of normal hand lay-up moulding.

A continuous thread of glass
This can be wound round the component being impregnated with the resin as it proceeds. This filament winding process produces high-performance components such as pressure piping, but is limited in form and expensive to set up.

Other reinforcement materials have been developed which give improved properties, albeit at increased cost. These are Carbon Fibre, a crystalline fibre developed by the Royal Aircraft Establishment in 1963, with a strength and modulus superior to that of glass fibre, and Aramid Fibre, a lightweight, low modulus fibre developed by Du Pont Industrial Fibres, under the trademark of Kevlar.

Fabrication – the mould

The process of fabrication involves laying up successive layers of resin into which glass fibre reinforcement is embedded to follow a mould profile (see Fig. 2.2). Reid and O'Brien (1973) have described the basic laying-up techniques. The open mould 'contact process' uses either hand lay-up or spray-up application. There are, in addition, some other mechanised processes such as 'press moulding' (hot or cold), using matching moulds to press out panels so that both sides of the panel have moulded surfaces. The moulds for this process are expensive and are more difficult to adapt to accommodate variations in panel shape. Other processes use 'resin-injected techniques', where the glass fibre

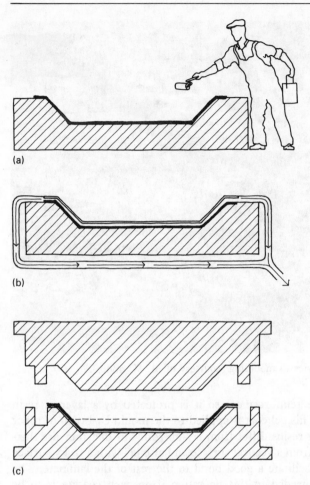

Fig. 2.2 Methods of GRP fabrication: (a) contact moulding; (b) vacuum moulding; (c) press moulding.

reinforcement is placed in a mould of the required shape and resin is forced under pressure, or a combination of pressure and vacuum, into the mould space.

Hand lay up or contact process
The simplest and most common method of building up the reinforcement and resin is by the hand lay-up technique. Firstly, the mould is waxed and polished using a non-silicone based wax (see Fig. 2.3). It is usually sufficient to do this once every three to five usages of the mould. A release agent, the most common type being polyvinyl alcohol (PVAL), is then applied over the entire surface of the mould and allowed to dry thoroughly. When the mould has been 'run in', it is possible to do away with this operation, except at the edges, relying only on the waxed surface for separation.

The durability of a moulding is mainly dependent on its surface. Moisture

Fig. 2.3   Mould waxing prior to moulding (courtesy of M. Wigmore).

will attack the glass fibre reinforcement so it is protected by a layer of resin known as the 'gel coat'. This gel coat is applied to the mould by brush or roller at 450–600 g/m². Gel coat resins differ from lay-up resins in that they are thixotropic to avoid draining from a vertical surface and also gel with a tacky surface where exposed to air to facilitate a good bond to the rest of the laminate. The utmost care and skill is needed in this operation if an even coating is to be achieved without the entrainment of air bubbles or trapping of dirt. The thickness should be carefully controlled, for where the coating is in excess of 600 μm thick, crazing and cracking, coupled with reduced impact resistance in use, is likely to occur. Faults in the surface of the gel coat will result in water penetration and a subsequent breakdown of the glass fibre reinforcement leading to swelling and rupture of the laminate.

For a small moulding, mixing is done by the laminator using a volume-measuring device to measure in the catalyst. In the simplest case it is done by hand. Where larger volumes are required, measuring and mixing would be done by a machine in a separate area under the charge of a responsible person.

The lay-up of the glass fibre reinforcement and resin can start as soon as the gel coat has hardened sufficiently not to come away on the finger when touched. The resin is mixed as before and a liberal coat is applied over the gel coat. The optimum quantity of lay-up resin can be calculated from the weight of glass reinforcement. For chopped strand mat the resin : glass ratio should be between

2.5 : 1 and 2 : 1 by weight. The first layer of reinforcement is pressed into the mould and consolidated with a brush or roller. The lay-up is consolidated with a roller and subsequent layers of resin and glass mat are applied until the required thickness is built up. Fig. 2.4 shows rolling out the lay-up to remove air bubbles.

Fig. 2.4 Rolling out the lay-up to remove air bubbles (courtesy of M. Wigmore).

Spray lay-up

An alternative method of building up the resin and reinforcement in the contact moulding procedure is by the simultaneous deposition of resin and chopped glass fibre by spray moulding equipment. Spray lay-up considerably reduces the labour content in the process, although rolling out is still required to consolidate the laminate and ensure the resin is mixed.

Machine moulding

There are several methods of producing GRP mouldings by more mechanised methods than the contact moulding technique described so far. These mechanised processes such as 'resin injection', 'vacuum forming' and pultrusion (only applicable to long continuous runs) are not normally relevant to cladding units. This is partly because of the limits of size possible with these processes and partly because of the capital investment in the necessary machinery. Cladding panels are not often produced in long continuous runs and, because architects are normally designing a one-off panel system requiring only a few hundred panels, the capital outlay for relatively sophisticated machinery becomes inapplicable. One of the few exceptions to this would be the roof panels for Covent Garden Market, London, which were produced by Armshire Reinforced Plastics using resin injection and pressing techniques (see Holloway (1975) p. 69).

It is interesting to make a comparison with the boat building industry, where this 'tooling up' process is done once and is paid for by the production of a large number of products. In cladding this would require a complete development programme every time a new contract is initiated. Glass reinforced polyester being a complex design material leads to development methods whereby the manufacture and testing of a prototype is carried out before starting the production run. Boat construction, being mainly a mass production process, can allow extensive development time for this process to take place, whereas building components, such as cladding, are often subcontracted, there being a short time between the design and requirement of the product, putting the manufacturer under considerable pressure to meet specific deadlines in relation to other design work and construction processes. Hand lay-ups and spray techniques are slow; the production of one panel per day per mould is the norm, causing the manufacturer to use a number of moulds to meet the requirement. This, in turn, increases costs, coupled with the fact that a mould may only last 50–100 panels, after which it would have to be discarded.

The mould

Before an item can go into production a considerable amount of work has to be done to prepare the mould required for its manufacture. The quality of the mould will ultimately dictate the quality of the finished product. For most projects where a number of panels are required the moulds are formed of GRP. Master patterns can be made in materials such as timber, steel or plaster, from which this GRP mould is taken. A GRP laminate during curing may shrink by 0.1–0.4 per cent (linearly), and as there are two moulding processes between the pattern and the finished product, the net shrinkage may be as much as 0.8 per cent. (One manufacturer gave as an example a 9 m long panel being oversized by 1.2 mm to allow for shrinkage.) The manufacturer gradually knows from experience how much to allow for shrinkage, depending upon the shape of the unit, the resin and the temperature change expected. Once the mean dimension has been established, the deviations from the mean would be relatively small. The extent to which the fabricator of a timber master pattern allows for this shrinkage is a skill learned through experience. Tooling is one of the highest costs in GRP manufacture. Moulders and finishers are considered to be skilled labour and most of the larger manufacturers have introduced training schemes for apprentices to this trade.

Because of the bespoke nature of the industry and the number of panels involved for each job, the manufacturers cannot afford too many prototypes before a satisfactory target dimension is achieved. A large number of panels will have to be produced from a number of moulds, not all necessarily to the same master pattern. This is a factor affecting manufacturing deviations of panel size (tolerances).

Another difficulty of manufacture is that some of the stresses set up in the matrix are inherent, produced by the differential shrinkage between fibre and resin when the GRP composite is cooled to room temperature during fabrication, as a result of differing coefficients of thermal expansion ($70-100 \times 10^{-6}/°C$ for resin versus $5.0 \times 10^{-6}/°C$ for glass). Resin additives can alleviate these effects by reducing shrinking.

Although it is clearly desirable to design for simple moulds, it is possible to develop 'split moulds' with movable sections to achieve return angles. A flash line is then seen on the face of the panel at the junction of the two sections of the mould. It is possible to 'buff' this out in finishing operations or render it less obvious by designing the 'split' to coincide with a change of profile. It is vital that reasonable access be given to the fabricator in order to lay up evenly all sections of the mould and to facilitate consolidation of the material by means of a hand roller to expel any air bubbles which may be entrained in the laminate. Too large a mould and one also of a complicated shape means that the fabricator cannot get to all the areas in order to lay up an even coating of glass fibre and resin, while at the same time ensuring good compaction and ease of rolling out. The ideal panel width is one where the operator can reach all parts of the mould easily, say 2 m wide. The domed panels at Castle Park, Nottingham (architects: Nicholas Grimshaw Partnership) were manufactured as one-piece units using a tilting mould allowing access to all areas for the fabricator. These tilting moulds are similar to those used in boat production (Fig. 2.5).

Quality control and faults in curing

Because the GRP panel industry has a high labour content, the designer/ purchaser is totally dependent upon the quality of the labour force employed and the conditions under which they work in the factory. Environmental control on the shop floor is very important in terms of evenness in temperature and constant relative humidity if the final product is going to be lasting and of good quality. For an illustration of a typical production process, see Fig. 2.6.

Although in its simplest form the laying up in layers of glass fibre looks easy, the process leading to the successful application in large wall elements is much more complicated. There is the initial difficulty of choosing a resin to make a laminate by reference to the resin properties alone. The properties and performance required of the whole matrix must be considered for different resins and their additives will perform different functions with regard to weathering, flame retardance and colour stability. Depending upon choice, these various constituents may be used in different proportions to each other, and the right control of temperature and humidity limits are essential. The temperature in the workshop should be controlled between 18 °C and 25 °C and ideally maintained overnight. The workshop should not be damp, as this causes the glass rein-

Fig. 2.5 Tilting moulds being used for boat production (courtesy of M. Wigmore).

Fig. 2.6 View of the Anmac factory. Note separate reinforcement area.

forcement to soak up water and could lead to delamination of the finished article and a breaking up of the resin/glass fibre matrix. Cleanliness is of importance, as any contamination in the lay-up will degrade appearance and strength, while good ventilation is also a necessity in order to control styrene content in the atmosphere.

Cutting catalyst levels and low workshop temperatures will produce inferior laminates which perform badly. Blemishes can include gel-coat wrinkling, surface pin-holing, poor adhesion of the gel coat and resin, spotting of the gel-coat surface, striation in pigment flotation, pattern of fibres visible through a gel coat, patches of pale colour or 'fish-eyes', blisters, crazing of surface of resin and star cracking when gel coat is too thick, internal dry patches, poor wetting of the mat and leaching after leaving glass fibre exposed to moisture.

As the performance and durability of the GRP product depends mainly on the cure of the polyester resin, it is essential that there should be some means of establishing whether or not the laminate is suspect. Such a method is recommended in Appendix A of BS 4549, Part I: 1979 *Guide to quality control requirements for reinforced plastic mouldings*, the 'Barcol Test', which is a form of impact test.

The weight of the laminate measured against that of the requirements laid down in the specification will give a check as to whether a layer of reinforcement has been omitted, while the Barcol Test for hardness, although not giving an absolute measurement of the cure, will differentiate between a really bad laminate and a reasonable one with a little more accuracy than is possible by casual observation. The laminate should have a hardness of around 35 within a few days. Post-curing for 16 hours at 40 °C can improve this to around 40 with decreased water absorption and little effect on the other mechanical properties. Test laminates can be used to check the strength of a specified lay-up, although these may not necessarily be representative of the overall quality achieved in the product.

The heat distortion point for GRP is particularly important for cladding applications where high external temperatures are expected, for example, the use of dark-coloured panels in south-facing elevations. For such applications resins with higher heat distortion points must be used, while it is vital that test and post-curing are carried out at or above temperatures the panel may sustain in use. Any creep in the material that can be anticipated can be taken into account in the design by adding stiffeners to the panel.

To achieve a quality product, therefore, it is necessary for the panel to be manufactured in the right conditions, by experienced workers, in the correct proportion, using the right techniques. Ignorance of these controls may lead to what appears to be a satisfactory product on the shop floor, but one that is unlikely to perform satisfactorily throughout its expected design life. All this leads to a situation where great care has to be taken in quality control during production. It is not outside the designer's field to be able to set out these conditions in his specification, and it is essential to request from the manufacturer record sheets for each unit produced. Manufacturers should, therefore, be asked if they:

(a) Keep a record sheet for each unit manufactured, containing a unique reference number, date of casting, mix details, tests carried out, etc.
(b) Check weighing of each unit after curing.
(c) Have an established procedure for dealing with minor blemishes and defects discovered in the units at various stages.

Some specifiers have found it necessary to have direct quality control over all the units during manufacture. The specification for the works and materials at Mondial House, for example, includes a clause that 'each panel will be inspected dimensionally, and for gel surface defects and signs of poor laminating, by the consultants and marked if approved'. The GRP panels for the Herman Miller factory at Bath were also inspected individually by the architects, Farrell and Grimshaw, in the factory. Although this may still be necessary for prestige jobs, most reputable manufacturers will now have the correct quality control procedures. Indeed, it could be said that architects' standards for cladding are higher than can be reasonably expected, and it is interesting to reflect that GRP-coffered slab formers are often acceptable with lower standards of workmanship.

GRP cladding in use

The first applications of GRP in the building industry were in the mid 1950s when there was intense design activity in the material. In 1956 the Monsanto 'House of the Future' was exhibited at Disneyland, making revolutionary use of structural GRP. By 1961 the technology had been advanced to the point where GRP foam sandwich buildings had been erected as relay rooms for British Railways (Anon., 1961) (see Fig. 2.7), and the system extended to produce a research laboratory in the Antarctic. In 1966 pressed GRP panels with a concrete backing were produced by the Indulex Engineering Company for a multi-storey block of flats in Paddington, London, known as the SF1 System (Building Research Association of New Zealand, 1981). With this rapid advance in the application of the material, it is not surprising that many people expected a breakthrough in the advance of GRP structures leading to the widespread use of the material in building. This breakthrough has never really come about. Glass reinforced polyester has, however, established itself in some less wide-ranging areas of building construction, the premier one being the manufacture of cladding panels.

The simplicity of the manufacturing process allowed many small fabricators to set up without the need for large capital expenditure. There are, however, only a handful who specialise in cladding and have had experience of large contracts. Major building projects in the UK using GRP cladding panels include:

Fig. 2.7   Early use of GRP panels for British Railways relay rooms.

GLC SF1 Tower Blocks	1966	Indulex
HMS Raleigh, Plymouth	1973	H. H. Robertson
Olivetti buildings at Haslemere	1974	Anmac
Mondial House, London	1975	Anmac and Brensal
Nine Elms Flower Market, London	1975	Armshire Reinforced Plastics
American Express building, Brighton	1977	Brensal
Herman Miller factory, Bath	1977	Artech Plastics

A designer wishing to use GRP as a cladding material, even now, twenty-five years after it was first used, is liable to face some difficulties. R. D. Gay (1965) at the Conference on Plastics in Building Structures stated:

> The data on properties of these materials do not exist in the form required – the plastics industry has not learned to present them in that way; some data are not yet available because the professions have not made known what they require and how. There are no codes of practice and no textbooks are available for the design of building structures.

The situation has improved since that time. Articles have appeared in journals explaining the nature of the material and the principles of detailing (Reid and O'Brien, 1973, 1974). These, in addition to handbooks from the leading resin and reinforcement manufacturers (Scott Bader, 1980) and several conferences on the subject (Holloway, 1978; Scott Bader, 1979) have gone a long way to give the interested architect a good insight into the design of panels. The manufacturers of glass fibre reinforcement give brief design techniques and performance figures for given laminates and sections (Fibreglass Ltd, 1977c). Design guides for the engineering design of GRP laminates are available, if somewhat rare. One of the most comprehensive documents on this subject is a 200-page section on the design of laminates in Gibbs and Cox Inc. (1960). The engineering principles used are not new, but the analysis required to understand a 'one-off' moulding is a complex engineering problem.

Standardisation of components

Because of its mouldability GRP is often marketed offering a variety of shapes and sizes and many manufacturers' catalogues stress its versatility of shape. Even so, economies of production can only be really achieved with standardised identical units.

Manufacturers' moulds are high cost items and repetitive identical units are desirable for maximum economy, although this similarity need not extend to uniformity of colour.

Specials or non-standard units increase costs and involve the structural engineer in numerous adjustments in the design of the fixings. Curved or shaped panels need special moulds.

If special units are to be incorporated it is an advantage if they are smaller than the standard-sized panel used in the majority of the scheme, for it is much easier to adapt the original mould than to have to make a new one for four or five specials. Gillingham Marina is a good example of the use of adaptable moulds using the same basic shape with filler pieces for door and window panels (see Brookes and Ward (1981), p. 1137).

Strangely, although we tend to associate the boat building industry with one-off large boat designs, Wigmore (1981) has shown that the reasons why GRP is widely used for boats is that the production of large numbers of identical products pays for the initial tooling up and capital expenditure in such items as rotating moulds.

Fire resistance

In the UK a Class O resistant laminate to BS 476 is required for claddings on buildings above 15 m high, or Class 2 or 3, within 1 m of the boundary. In order to provide this degree of fire resistance, it has been usual to improve the fire retardancy of polyester resins by:

1. The addition of fillers.
2. The use of additives, such as antimony oxide plus chlorinated paraffin, which can be mixed with the resin.
3. By building in certain groups in the chemical structure of the resin, for example, dibromoneopentyl glycol, hexochloro-endomethylene tetrahydrophthalic acid, chlorostyrene.

It has been found, however, that the weathering qualities of the laminate produced in this way are reduced in positions exposed to ultraviolet rays and even white will mellow with age.

An additional way is to coat the internal surface of the GRP structure with an intumescent coating. Intumescent polyesters are now available which contain compounds designed to give a carbonaceous foam on application of a flame. However, all methods so far used in trying to improve the fire retardance of polyester resins have considerably lowered the GRP's resistance to breakdown (loss of gloss, colour change) when exposed to the outdoor environment. Tests have shown that on one common type of fire-retardant GRP sheet, using tetra-chlorophthalic acid polyester as an inhibitor, the surface deterioration was 2.5 to 3.0 times faster than sheets based on general purpose/conventional polyester resins.

Another solution to the problem of providing the required fire rating has been to apply a two-pack polyurethane surface coating in order to protect the laminate from the effects of ultraviolet light, for example An-o-clad by Anmac Ltd. This uses a modified gel-coat system which in itself adds to the fire characteristics of the panel and is then coated with the two-pack polyurethane to give good weatherability. This system when tested to BS 476 Part 7 for a Class 1 test had 'nil' spread of flame on the test samples. Good resistance to the breakdown of the gel coat is also achieved by coating the GRP sheets with a lacquer based on an ultraviolet stabilised acrylic resin.

A more usual solution is either to position the building away from the boundary, or ask for a relaxation to the Class O fire requirement. In this case a general purpose 'isophthalic' gel coat can be used, which itself has no fire-retardant characteristics, but which protects the laminating resin containing the fire-retardant additive from ultraviolet light. But, of course, it does not get a Class O fire rating. When applying for such a waiver it may be necessary for tests to be carried out which simulate in-service conditions on full panels, including the appropriate jointing technique used. The configuration and design of the joints must significantly affect the performance of the panels during a fire. The panels for Mondial House (see Fig. 2.8), designed by Peter Hodge Associates, and manufactured by Anmac Ltd and Brensal Plastics Ltd, were tested by Yarsley Laboratories. Two sets of fire tests were performed, the first on tested coupons in accordance with BS 476, the second on two complete panels with a joint, set up in the attitude to be used in service. A large gas flame with heat output of

Fig. 2.8   Mondial House, London (architects: Hubbard Ford and Partners) (courtesy of Scott Bader Co. Ltd).

190 W/min was set up beneath the bottom of the panels. The results of the test showed that there was not uncontrolled spread of flame over the surface and even after an hour's exposure the panel still retained its form.

Incidentally, this project is probably the largest structure erected using GRP cladding in the UK and the inclusion of a mini-rib finish to these panels has resulted in them only now having to be washed down after seven years since initial installation.

Thus, the two main problems associated with GRP, that of weathering, especially as a result of ultraviolet degradation, and fire resistance, tend to work against each other. The addition of fillers and pigments to reach some sort of fire resistance acceptability through tests laid down in the building regulations tends to weaken the material's capacity to resist weathering and a darkening of the surface pigments may take place.

Weathering

The selection of colour can significantly affect the overall weatherability of the panels. In general, the stronger colours, such as oranges and reds, have a tendency to fade under the effect of ultraviolet light; the ultraviolet light will cause the surface of the material to chalk. Architects often specify these colours in ignorance of the problems associated with some pigments, and all too often the manufacturers will supply the colours as requested. Present fashion for oranges, browns and reds has exaggerated this difficulty which, by the way, is not confined to GRP claddings.

In general, colouring of GRP panels is best done by pigment in the resin or gel coat and not as an applied finish. However, Blaga (1978) claims that good resistance to the effects of moisture and/or temperature-induced stress fatigue is achieved by coating the GRP sheets with a lacquer based on ultraviolet-stabilised acrylic resin.

> The acrylic coating protects the glass-resin interface against the effects of stress fatigue and the underlying matrix against the action of UV light. This type of coating may be particularly useful for fire resistant GRP sheets which are especially susceptible to breakdown in outdoor exposure. Similarly GRP sheets protected with a UV stabilised (in-plant laminated) PVF surfacing film (0.025 mm thick) have remarkable resistance to the effect of weathering.

The difficulty may be to achieve a permanent bond between the laminate and this polyvinyl fluoride film (Tedlar).

No completely satisfactory method of assessing weathering resistance of plastics materials in service by laboratory simulation has yet been found. Weatherometer testing and Xenon arc testing (Reference ISO R.879: 1968) are popular methods, but these can, at most, only give an indication of performance in use. After 1000 hours, exposure to the 'Xenon test' any change of colour should be moderate and uniform.

Colour fastness tends to be uniform within any one batch of panels, but can vary from batch to batch. One method of anticipating differences in colour fastness between panels is to use a striped effect as at the Olivetti factory, Haslemere (architect: James Stirling) (see Fig. 2.9). The colour of the outer skin can also increase any possibility of delamination of sandwich panels due to temperature build-up on the surface. The darker the colour and the higher the temperature, the greater the risk of delamination. Interior use of GRP is usually successful.

In theory, minor blemishes in GRP can be made good on-site, provided that there are correct weather conditions and highly skilled labour force available. In practice such conditions hardly ever exist and, as yet, methods of curing on-site are not available. Thus normally the panels are returned to the factory for repair. To prevent accidental damage on-site, it is important to protect the panels during assembly. Panels for Herman Miller, for example, were protected with a plastic coating while being installed (see Fig. 2.10).

Surface scratching, which can be caused by something as simple as a window cleaner's ladder that has no padded protection, produces unsightly defects. The client should be warned to guard against this during maintenance. There may be some cases where the back of the panel is exposed to the weather (i.e. balustrades), in this case care must be taken to apply a gel coat to both sides of the panel. Condensation on the back face of a panel which has no gel-coat protection on its inner skin can also lead to premature breakdown of the laminate if the glass fibres are exposed at the surface.

51

Fig. 2.9   Olivetti training centre at Haslemere (architects: James Stirling) (courtesy of Scott Bader Co. Ltd)

Surface finish

Large shiny surfaces in GRP will show warping when used extensively over large, flat elevations. Panels up to 1 m wide can be accommodated with a high gloss, but over that width surface ripple may become apparent. This is not only a problem of GRP – even plate glass and aluminium sheeting suffers in this respect. For this reason, some surface treatment may be appropriate, such as a matt-textured finish. Within reason the coarser the texture the more surface deflection it will accommodate. On the other hand, if the texture becomes too coarse it can slow down the rate of lamination, increasing the cost of production. Probably the optimum finish is a riven slate texture created in the master pattern mould, which has all the advantage of accommodating surface deflection, while at the same time being economical to laminate. However, riven slate has the advantage that it is limited in its size and therefore it has to be panelled – though this does not necessarily create difficulties if designed with care.

Vinyl cloth is very good for producing a light striated panel. For example, panels for a store in Nottingham shown under construction (see Fig. 2.11) were

Fig. 2.10   Panels at the Herman Miller factory, Bath (architects: Farrell and Grimshaw) (courtesy of Jo Reid and John Peck).

Fig. 2.11 Nottingham Co-op under construction (courtesy of Anmac Ltd).

produced with a matt surface after laying vinyl wallpaper on to the mould from which the production mould is manufactured. However, against this, vinyl cloth is only available in set widths with resulting difficulties in hiding the joints. Random spray-on textures have advantages when compound curves are a feature of the design.

It is not uncommon, because of the ease of moulding GRP panels, that they are used in conjunction with other materials for solving special corner or flashing details. For example, at the factory at Winwick Quay, Warrington (architects:

Fig. 2.12 Corner panels at Winwick Quay, Warrington (architects: Nicholas Grimshaw Partnership).

Nicholas Grimshaw Partnership) (see Fig. 2.12), GRP corner panels are painted to match the silver-grey 'alucobond' aluminium sandwich panels. This mixing of materials can lead to problems of colour matching and difference in rates of colour change.

Panel stiffening

Glass reinforced polyester has a high tensile strength but low modulus of elasticity. Although it can accept quite high loads, this is only done at the expense of great deformation or deflection. High deflections are undesirable as they can result in gel-coat cracking. Because of the cost of the material, thickening of the laminate overall would be too expensive. Four basic ways of stiffening panels in common use are shown in Fig. 2.13. These are:

(a) Shaped profiles.
(b) Ribbed construction.
(c) Sandwich construction with foamed core.
(d) Sandwich construction with sheet core.

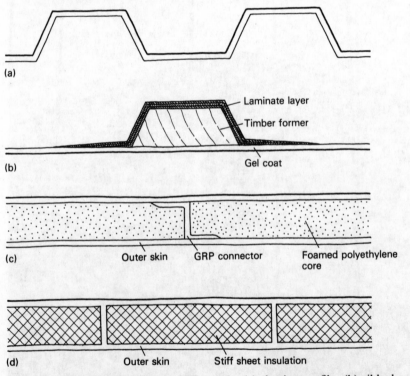

Fig. 2.13 Methods of stiffening GRP panels: (a) shaping profile; (b) ribbed construction; (c) sandwich construction – GRP connector and foamed insulation core; (d) sandwich construction – stiff insulation sheet laid into lamination.

Shaped profiles

Panels can be designed for stiffness in a geometric form. Even for a nominally flat panel, a shallow profile, pyramid, dome or dish, can make a considerable improvement to its stiffness. In some cases it may be possible to design the panels so that the form for stiffening also acts structurally. For example, the spandrel panels at the American Express new European Headquarters building at Brighton (architects: GMW Partnership), which are 7.2 m × 1.4 m × 0.8 m

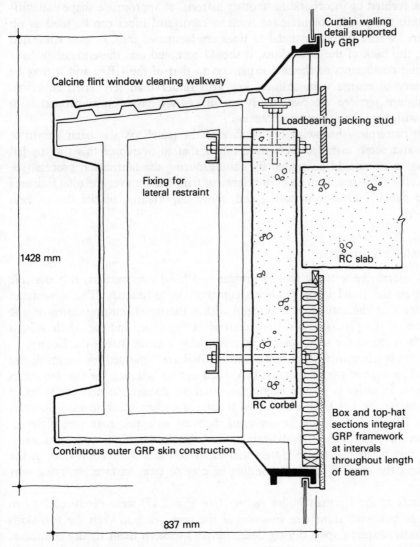

Fig. 2.14 Section through GRP loadbearing panels at American Express building, Brighton (architects: Collins Melvin Ward Partnership). *NB* panels 7200 mm long.

Class II, GRP channel sections, not only form the cladding, but also act as structural elements supporting the glazing above (see Fig. 2:14).

Ribbed construction

Single-skin construction can be stiffened by a system of ribs on the back of the panel, such as those at Mondial House, London (see Fig. 2.15). Ribs are normally made from GRP laminated over a rib former in a mould, but they can also be formed by incorporating another material of appropriate shape and stiffness into the panel. Polyurethane foam or cardboard tubes can be used as rib formers. Where timber or metal sections are laminated into, or over-laminated on to, the back of the GRP skins, it should be noted that these materials have differing coefficients of thermal expansion to that of the GRP, and it may be necessary to ensure a mechanical key grip rather than rely upon adhesion. Aluminium sections are particularly useful as they have similar properties to GRP with regard to thermal expansion.

Rib patterning/shadowing on the face of the panel has also been known to occur and some manufacturers have found that to overcome this the top-hat section or rib should be vented by cutting during the fabrication process (see Fig. 2.16). This results in an even balance of temperature over the total face area of the panel, both during curing and, more importantly, on-site due to heat build-up.

Sandwich construction

As an alternative to using shaped profiles or ribbed construction, it is possible to stiffen the panel using sandwich construction techniques. The advantages here are that the insulation is integral within the panel, cutting down on the number of site processes involved, thereby saving time, and the whole skin is manufactured to the same tolerances and quality control within the factory.

In sandwich construction two skins of GRP are separated by an insulating core. The edge of the panel must be carried out by bringing the two laminates together. In order to ensure maximum structural connection between skins, it is customary to use GRP connectors at intervals when using foamed polyurethane. Problems do occur, however, in choosing an appropriate core material, and serious defects through delamination of the insulative core from the panel itself may occur due to the differential expansion and contraction rates of the skin and the core. With poor bonding of core to face, surface blistering may occur.

Panels at the Herman Miller factory (see Fig. 2.17) were produced by two separate sandwich skins, the function of the core being to keep the two skins a constant distance apart during deflection and to keep them rigidly connected so that they act as a composite element.

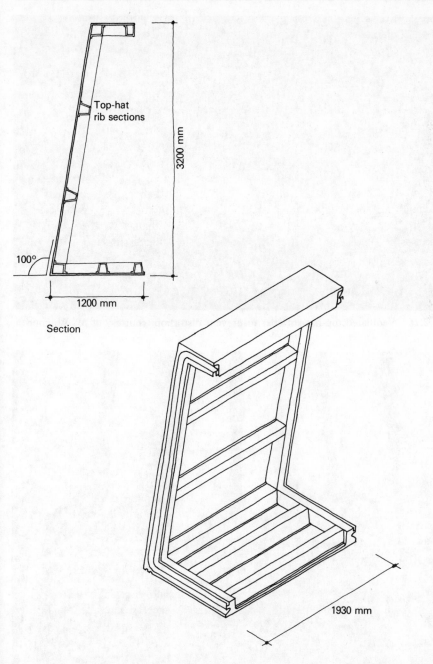

Top-hat
rib sections

3200 mm

100°

1200 mm

Section

1930 mm

Fig. 2.15 Stiffening of GRP panels at Mondial House, London, using GRP top-hat and box sections (architects: Hubbard Ford and Partners).

Fig. 2.16   Ventilated top-hat stiffener to prevent distortion (courtesy of M. Wigmore).

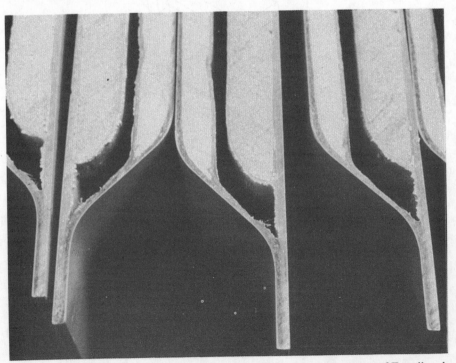

Fig. 2.17   Sandwich panels as used at the Herman Miller factory (courtesy of Farrell and Grimshaw).

Jointing

Most problems of jointing GRP cladding panels occur at the external panel to panel joint, particularly at the cross-over situation. These external joints and their jointing materials must be able to accommodate the thermal movements and deflection movements of the mouldings under maximum dead and live load conditions, as well as allowing for manufacturing tolerances and errors in erection.

Three types of joints are commonly used:
(a) Mastic sealant joints.
(b) Gasket joints.
(c) Open-drained joints.

Mastic sealant joints

The performance of this type of joint depends on the skill of site applicator. There have been a number of examples of sealant failures with GRP panels. For example, the *Architects' Journal* (Reid and O'Brien, 1974) reported on two projects, HMS Sealand and British Gas Corporation, Solihull, where joints between panels showed unsightly mastic failure. This type of failure is often due to insufficient account being taken of the expected thermal and moisture movement at the design stage and, in some cases, caused by failure to remove all traces of releasing agent at the panel edge before sealant is applied. Recent developments in silicone rubbers have improved the performance of sealants because of their much greater movement accommodation and lower stress at the bond face.

Gasket joints

This type of joint normally incorporates a neoprene-extruded section which, because they are factory produced, are not so dependent on the site operative for their successful application. As an alternative to neoprene, Ethylene Propylene Diamine Monomer (EPDM) has better inherent resistance to oxidation attack and subsequent ageing. However, its drawback is poor resistance to attack from lubricating oils and various solvents. EPDM's ability to recover from compression is also less than neoprene. Although it is possible, according to their formulation to obtain rubbers with good or bad tear resistance in both neoprene or EPDM, generally speaking EPDM has less resistance to tearing than neoprene and thus is less easy to handle on-site.

Site bonding of neoprene sections is now quite common for cross-over joints. For example, the neoprene gasket joint used at the Herman Miller factory (see Fig. 2.18) was a simple glazing technique for both vertical and horizontal joints. A top-hat section is screwed into an aluminium carrier system which in turn is supported by the main framing. A continuous gasket is then pushed into this top-hat section. At parapet level the neoprene vertical joint changes to a narrower mastic sealant, due to difficulties in carrying the top-hat section over the curved jointing profile.

Neoprene gaskets work best when they are compressed within the joint, normally on the back side of the panel edge profile. A simple compressible gasket

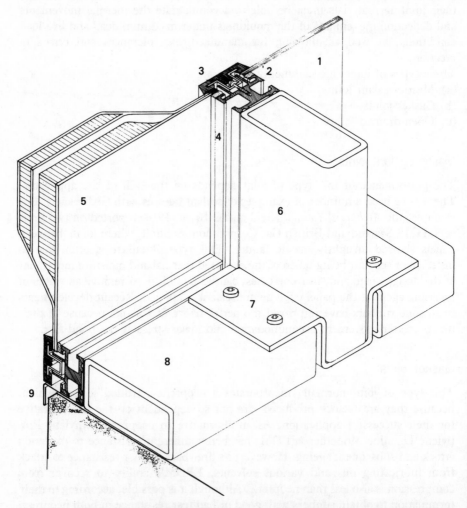

Fig. 2.18 Neoprene jointing gaskets used at the Herman Miller factory, Bath. (1) 6 mm surface-modified solar control glass. (2) Resilient packing strip. (3) Continuous neoprene gasket fitted to 'U'-shaped aluminium beading screwed back to carrier. (4) Extruded aluminium carrier screwed back to steel hollow section. (5) GRP sandwich panel. Overall thickness 75 mm. Outer insulation 19 mm polyurethane foam. Inner insulation 25 mm polyurethane foam. (6) 127 mm × 63.5 mm hollow section steel subframe mullion. (7) 6 mm mild steel assembly shoe bolted to concrete slab. (8) 127 mm × 63.5 mm hollow section steel horizontal rail. (9) Pressed aluminium cill fixed back behind carrier. (architects: Farrell and Grimshaw) (courtesy of D. Cousans).

using timber edging pieces with GRP panels was developed for Teeside Polytechnic (architects: Basil Spence) (see Fig. 2.19), for use with panels 1 m × 1 m. A more complicated gasket joint was developed for Mondial House (see Hodge 1968 and Fig. 2.20), which uses a combination of a neoprene baffle, a PVC back channel and a strip sealant under compression from a back plate. The joint was tested successfully by Yarsley Laboratories, to BS 4315 simulating 18.75 cm of rain per hour at a wind speed of 56–64 km/h. This very sophisticated joint combines the principles of an open-drained joint with that of a labyrinth joint. As a result of this experience at Mondial House, Anmac Ltd have their own 'patented' two-stage mechanical joint called LSB (see Fig. 2.21). This has the advantage that the jointing product is under compression and hidden from ultraviolet light.

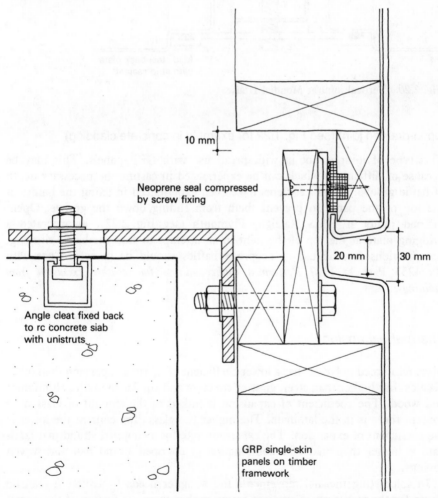

10 mm

Neoprene seal compressed
by screw fixing

20 mm   30 mm

Angle cleat fixed back
to rc concrete siab
with unistruts

GRP single-skin
panels on timber
framework

Fig. 2.19 Joints between panels at Teeside Polytechnic (architects: Basil Spence and Partners).

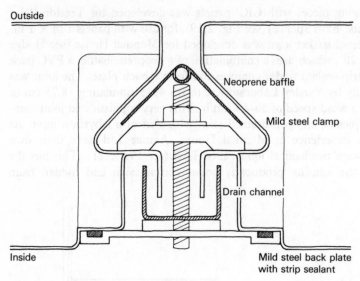

Outside

Neoprene baffle

Mild steel clamp

Drain channel

Inside

Mild steel back plate
with strip sealant

Fig. 2.20 Vertical joint at Mondial House.

Open-drained joint (see Fig. 1.22 for example in concrete cladding)

This type of joint is not in widespread use with GRP panels. This may be because of difficulties which can be experienced in casting the necessary depth of baffle groove. Other problems have been experienced in fixing the baffles at the top of the panel to prevent them from sliding down the groove. Open-drained joints at HMS Raleigh, Plymouth (see Fig. 2.22), incorporated a bridging plate at the top of the joint in an attempt to stop the baffle slipping. Specifications for the use of neoprene baffles should be in accordance with BS 4255 Part 1: 1967 *Performed rubber gaskets for weather exclusion from buildings.*

Thermal expansion

Glass reinforced polyester has a lower coefficient of thermal expansion than other plastics, but higher than steel, glass or concrete and similar to that of aluminium and wood. The coefficient of expansion is linked to the amount of glass fibre content there is in the laminate. The higher the glass fibre content the lower is the coefficient of expansion. The expansion rate for a chopped strand mat laminate is higher than that of a combination of chopped strand mat and woven rovings.

In calculating thermal movements the designer needs to assume a realistic figure for the temperature gradient set up within the cross-section of the panel. This will depend upon factors such as orientation, colour of cladding, any

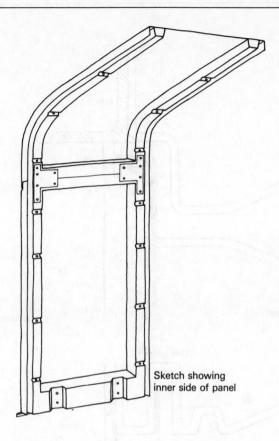

Sketch showing
inner side of panel

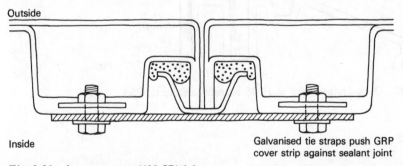

Outside

Inside

Galvanised tie straps push GRP
cover strip against sealant joint

Fig. 2.21   Anmac patent (400 SB) joint.

insulation that may be behind it (sandwich panel) and its fixing and jointing
aspects.

It is important to take account of thermal expansion in the design of fixings
at the interface of GRP panels and some other finish material or component
within the structure.

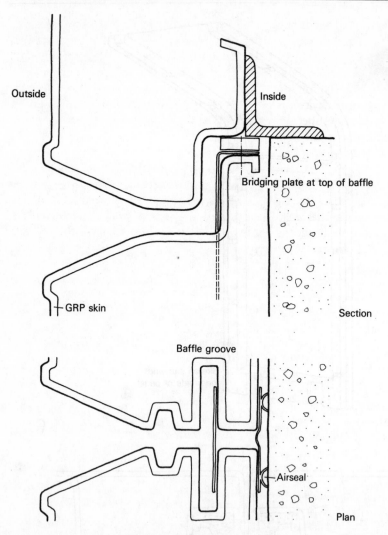

Outside

Inside

Bridging plate at top of baffle

GRP skin

Section

Baffle groove

Airseal

Plan

Fig. 2.22   Open-drained joint at HMS Raleigh (architects: PSA).

Fixings

It is obviously not possible to fit the panels on-site to an absolutely true and level structure. Tolerances on the base structure must be notified to the designer of the GRP panel system and reference should be made to BS 5606 which indicates the accuracy of assembly that may be expected on-site for given components and construction.

One of the difficulties of fixing any single-skin panel back to the supporting structure is the problem of restraining the fixing device within the thickness of the panel. Several methods have been tried, including fixing plates moulded into the backs of the panels incorporating bolt fixings. Most uses. however, depend upon a system of clamping the panel back to the structure, usually at the joint interface. The American Express building in Brighton uses this method (see Anon. 1977). Panels fixed at Mondial House incorporated a non-ferrous threaded fixing plate device hooked back on to the perimeter I-beam. The length of fixing involved resulted in this being an expensive way of achieving the necessary adjustment (see Fig. 2.23).

Generally speaking, panels should be fixed rigidly at one point, with all other fixings being designed to accommodate the movement likely to occur. The rigid fixing must in itself be able to be adjusted to accommodate the manufacturing and building tolerances (see BRE Digest 223 *Wall cladding: designing to minimise effects due to inaccuracies and movement*). Often designers allow for mild steel stiffeners within the flanges of GRP. If these are subsequently site drilled for bolt fixings and not treated or sealed, moisture penetration will lead to rusting and a delamination of the flanges.

The designer may need to consider fixings for handling – large panels are often difficult to handle on-site due to high wind speeds coupled with their own light weight, and the size and number of fixings for a large panel needs careful consideration.

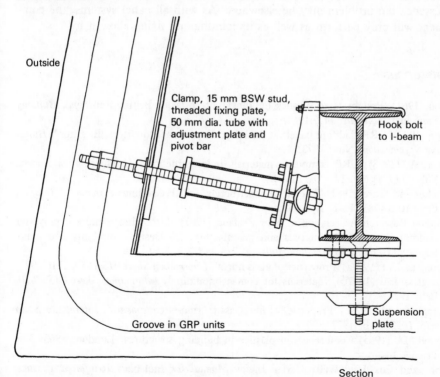

Section

Fig. 2.23   Fixing to I-beam at Mondial House (architects: Hubbard Ford & Partners)

Conclusion

It can be seen from the foregoing sections that the manufacture of successful GRP mouldings is far from the simple process which it may appear at first sight. Although in its simplest form laying-up layers of glass fibre is relatively easy, the process required to design and fabricate a product to satisfy its function for many years in a hostile environment is much more complicated. There are many types of resin and reinforcement types which can be modified by additives and fillers. The products have to be fabricated in the correct proportions by the right techniques and under the correct conditions to obtain a quality product.

Great care has to be taken in designing the correct stiffening of the panel using ribbed or sandwich construction, although more problems can associated with the latter. Jointing and fixings must be carefully considered to take account of any thermal movement and inaccuracies (spacing, plumb and alignment) of the structural supports, and detailed specifications of the required standards of manufacture, assembly and repair are essential.

Finally, specification of detailing, fixing and jointing is just as important as requirements for resins, pigment additives and types of glass fibre to be used. Many problems have, in the past, been attributed to the properties of GRP when in essence the problem may lie elsewhere. As with all panel systems, the component will only perform as well as its jointing and fixing allow it to.

References

Anon (1961) 'Prefabricated plastics buildings cut costs for British Railways', *Building Plant and Materials*, 11.5.1961.

Anon (1977) 'GRP cladding panels at American Express headquarters, Brighton', *Building Specification*, Nov. 1977.

Blaga, A. (1978) 'GRP composite materials in construction', *Industrialisation Forum*, Vol. 9 (1978) No. 1.

Brookes and Ward (1981) 'The art of construction – GRP claddings', *Architects' Journal*, Pt 1, 10.6.1981; Pt 2, 17.6.1981.

Building Research Association of New Zealand (1981) 'Glass fibre reinforced polyester cladding panels. (1) Materials and manufacture; (2) Design, durability and maintenance', *Building Information Bulletins*, 228 and 229, Sept. 1981.

Fibreglass Ltd (1977a) 'Properties of glass fibres', *Information Sheet FIS 1050*, Feb. 1977.

Fibreglass Ltd (1977b) 'Materials for contact moulding', *Information Sheet FIS 1030*, Feb. 1977.

Fibreglass Ltd (1977c) 'Properties of fibreglass thermoset composites', *Information Sheet FIS 1052*, Feb. 1977.

Gay, R. D. (1965) Conference on plastics in building structures, London, 1965. The Plastics Institute.

Gibbs and Cox Inc (1960) *Marine Design Manual for Fibreglass Reinforced Plastics*, McGraw-Hill Inc: London.

Hodge, P. (1968) *Glass Reinforced Resin for Structures*, Peter Hodge and Associates: London.

Holloway, L. (1975) *The Use of Plastics for Load Bearing and Infill Panels* (University of Surrey Symposium 1974), Manning Rapley: London.

Holloway, L. (1978) 'Design and specification of GRP cladding', RIBA Conference, Oct. 1978, Manning Rapley: London.

Reid and O'Brien (1973) 'Glass fibre reinforced plastics for buildings', *Architects' Journal*, 21.3.73; 4.4.73; 2.5.73.

Reid and O'Brien (1974) 'Principles of detailing GRP cladding', *Architects' Journal*, 18.9.74; 2.10.74; 16.10.74; 6.11.74.

Scott Bader Co. Ltd (1980) *Crystic Polyester Handbook*, Lund Humphries: London.

Scott Bader/Anmac/Fibreglass (1979) 'Designing with GRP' (Conference at Liverpool University 1979), *Building Specification*, Nov. 1979.

Wigmore M. (1981) 'Reinforced plastics – comparison of techniques used in boat and building construction', Liverpool University B.Arch. Dissertation.

Chapter 3

Glass fibre reinforced cement

Introduction

Glass fibre reinforced cement is a composite material consisting of ordinary Portland cement, silica sand, and water, mixed with alkali-resistant glass fibres. The
development of these alkali-resistant glass fibres led to one of the most important
innovations in material technology for the building industry in recent years. It
was claimed that worldwide availability and relatively low cost of cement, coupled with the comparatively simple manufacturing processes involved, would
lead to its widespread use in cladding as an alternative to precast concrete
(Young, 1980). However, experience in use over the last few years has shown
that the use of stress factors in design still needs careful consideration and more
research is required into the nature of different mixes particularly when used
in composite panels with foamed insulation cores.

The material was developed in the late 1960s after pioneering studies at the
BRE led by Dr A. J. Majumdar, who successfully produced a fibre using glass-
containing zirconium oxide, which was capable of resisting alkali attack when
mixed with hydrating cement (see Building Research Establishment, 1974 and
1976). The Building Research Establishment's work was patented by the
National Research Development Council who approached Pilkington Bros. (St
Helens) to assist in the development of alkali-resistant fibres on a commercial
scale. By 1971 the fibre was being produced in quantity under the trade name
of Cem-Fil by Fibreglass Ltd, a Pilkington subsidiary, who have the worldwide
exclusive licence to exploit the new technology. In turn, in an attempt to ensure
the careful development of the GRC industry in terms of quality control and
design standards, Pilkington sells only to manufacturers who have an 'incorporation licence'. To date (1981), 100 UK companies and over 500 worldwide
have become licensees of Pilkington, although only a few of these are making
any serious attempt to market GRC cladding panels. Many manufacturers of
glass reinforced plastics and precast concrete also produce GRC components.

Like many new materials, its use was at first inhibited by lack of experience
in use and general rules governing design and adequate codes of practice. At
the international congress on glass fibre reinforced cement in London, 10–12
October 1979 (Glassfibre Reinforced Cement Association, 1980), although some

speakers complained of the lack of adequate standards, at the same conference M. W. Fordyce and D. Ward described moves towards standard specifications.

Over the last few years a number of major projects have been built using GRC. In the UK these would include the fire station at the National Exhibition Centre in Birmingham (Fig. 3.1), Fairfield West office complex in Kingston, the Scicon factory at Milton Keynes, Crédit Lyonnais building in London, factory built for UOP Fragrances Ltd. at Tadworth in Surrey (see Fig. 3.2), Melrose Centre in Milton Keynes, Newton Heath Library, Heathrow Euro-lounge, and the Royal Arsenal Co-op in Thanet, Kent, using the largest GRC panels to date (1981) in Europe. A large number of projects have also been built in the Middle East, Spain and Japan, and J. B. Ford (Glassfibre Reinforced Cement Association, 1980) has described twelve projects in the USA using GRC wall panels.

Design guidance is available describing the properties of glass reinforcement cement. A comprehensive description of the nature of this material and its manufacture has been published in the *Architects' Journal* (Young, 1978) in a four-part series, which commenced 15 February 1978. In this series John Young described the properties of GRC, its methods of manufacture and guidance on the specification and design of such factors as finishes, fixings and joints with reference to a number of case studies. (There is also a book version (Young, 1980).) A further *A.J.* article covering recent developments and feedback from practice by Brookes and Ward (1981). In addition to the *A.J.* series, Pilkington (1979) have produced excellent design guidance on the use of GRC, which includes a detailed description of such properties as its creep and stress-rupture, fatigue, density, thermal expansion, thermal conductivity and air and water permeance, with methods of design for determining working stresses, loading, thermal, acoustic and fire performance of a particular design. Information is also given on component testing, quality control and typical specifications. Designers intending to use the material in complicated shapes or in conjunction with composite insulation core materials should seek further advice from the manufacturers involved.

The material and its advantages

Glassfibre reinforced cement has been described by Young (1980) as 'an ideal marriage between brittle materials, cement, sand and glass, to produce a tough composite'. The most common percentage constitution of the material by weight is as follows:

Portland cement	40–60%
Water	20%
Sand	up to 25%
Glass fibre	5% (for spray techniques)
	3.5–4.5% (for premix)

Fig. 3.1 Fire station at the National Exhibition Centre (courtesy of GRC Ltd).

Fig. 3.2 UK headquarters for UOP Fragrances, Tadworth, Surrey (architects: Piano and Rogers) (courtesy of Brecht-Einzig).

The ultimate strength of GRC is essentially determined by the presence of the fibres and is, therefore, dependent upon the glass content, orientation of fibres, the degree of cure and the bonding of the fibres to the cement/sand matrix.

The glass fibre is introduced into the cement mix to carry the tensile forces, thus overcoming the main disadvantage of cement with its unreliable and relatively low tensile strength. The glass content controls the maximum loading the material can withstand, the impact performance and the durability of the composite. The incorporation of sand into the GRC mix helps to reduce shrinkage during drying out.

It can be seen that the glass fibres constitute only a small per cent by weight of the material and although, for example, fibres for GRC (Cem-fil) cost twice as much as fibres for GRP (£2000/tonne in 1981), the resultant material cost of a total 12 mm composite is only approx. half that of the material needed for an equivalent GRP composite. Having said that, of course, the material costs only represent a small percentage of the total costs, which will include overheads on production for more complicated panel shapes.

Glass fibre reinforced cement can be seen as an alternative to ordinary reinforced concrete in respect to its weather resistance, non-combustibility and low thermal movement. Advantage can be taken of its higher strength to weight ratio than other cementitious materials to produce strong, fire-resistant yet lightweight claddings. (Its strength to weight ratio is, however, less than GRP or metals.) Inevitably though, it is compared to GRP in respect to its method of manufacture and its resultant ability to be formed into a variety of shapes.

Cement when reinforced with glass fibre produces precast elements much thinner, typically 10 mm, than would be possible with traditional steel reinforced precast concrete, where 30 mm or more concrete cover to the steel is essential as protection against corrosion. Thinner sections are also made possible by the low water/cement ratio of the material, the lack of coarse aggregate, and its low permeability. As a result, panels of equal strength and function of precast concrete can be produced with thinner sections and therefore with less weight.

Whereas there is some difficulty in achieving Class O using GRP by the addition of fire-retardant additives, which have an adverse effect on weathering, with GRC the presence of cement, which is inherently non-combustible, makes it easier to obtain Class O fire resistance, depending upon the construction of the panel (see Table 3.3 showing relationship between wall construction and performance requirements).

The main disadvantage of GRC in comparison with precast concrete is that its structural properties of tensile strength and impact strength are reduced with age, although it is possible to show (Young, 1980) 'in all conditions of use, no component failures have been recorded up to twice the maximum recommended working stress values.'

Production methods

Process methods which have so far been developed for the fabrication of GRC components are 'spray' and 'premix'. Premix processes are those where the con-stituents are mixed together into a paste and subsequently formed by casting, press moulding or slip forming. Spray processes in which wet mortar paste and chopped glass fibre are simultaneously deposited from a dual spray-head into a suitable mould currently account for a large percentage of GRC production.

The properties of GRC premix are inherently different from, and usually inferior to, those of sprayed-up GRC due to more air being introduced into the mixture and less control over the fibre orientation. Thus for cladding panels spray processes are normally used. Three ways for spraying GRC are available:
1. Manual spray.
2. Mechanised spray.
3. Spray–dewater process.

Manual spray

Manual spraying is labour intensive, but offers the designer more flexibility in shape and profile than other methods of fabrication. Using the manual spray the operator moves the spray backwards and forwards across the mould surface until the required thickness of GRC, typically 10–12 mm, as opposed to an average 3–6 mm for GRP, is built up. Greater thickness tends to increase GRC pro-duction costs. As with GRP, the material can be built up locally around fixings and inserts, while roller compaction ensures total contact with the mould and removal of entrapped air. Roller compaction should be used after the first 3 mm layer has been sprayed to ensure a good surface finish. For an operator to spray effectively from either side of the mould a dimension of not more than 2 m width is recommended. For greater widths it is possible to erect some sort of working platform above the mould, but this makes spraying difficult and could affect the quality and cost of production. Fig. 3.3 shows manual spraying of GRC wall panels.

Mechanised spray

The hand spray can be easily mechanised for the production of simple flat com-ponents whereby the moulds are moved along a conveyor and pass below a boom on which the dual spray-head is mounted, moving to and fro to give uniform thickness and correct fibre distribution through the composite. The mechanical spray thus ensures greater consistency and more uniform thickness than the hand spraying. The restriction on width of the mould, as mentioned above, would also not apply. It has been shown possible to automate the manual spray method completely using computer-controlled robot units. However, the cost of mechanised spraying of complicated shapes and window openings becomes prohibitive unless continuous mass production runs are used, and so far these production methods are not used for one-off cladding designs in the UK.

Spray–dewater process

A variant of the mechanised spray process is the 'spray–dewater process' where the mould surface consists of a filter membrane through which excess water can be drawn off by vacuum immediately after spraying. The mechanical properties of the laminate are improved by the dewatering process which produces a denser composite.

A typical automatic spray–dewater plant for the continuous production of flat sheets consists of a mixer and pump conveying the GRC slurry to a slurry spray and glass chopper mounted on a traversing head. A conveyor belt passes the sprayed sheet through a finisher and vacuum box to draw off the excess water. After cutting and trimming, the 'green' sheet so produced can be removed, using a vacuum lift, in its limp state for post-forming into simple shapes. Although such production processes are used in the UK manufacturers tend to use dewatering processes only for the production of small flat units, such as wall or ceiling tiles, and find the manual spray methods more suitable for complex shapes.

Insulated panels

The inclusion of insulation between two skins of GRC is carried out in three main ways:

1. An insulating material such as PBAC (polystyrene bead aggregate concrete) can be placed, levelled and then additional GRC sprayed and compacted.
2. Panels of polystyrene may be placed in position and then covered with a slurry, or preformed webs of GRC used between the sheets of insulation to stiffen the panel.
3. Suitable foam may be injected between the two preformed skins of GRC. Foams include polyisocyanurate, polyurethane or phenolic. In the latter case internal webs of GRC are also used since the shear performance of the foam is inadequate.

For a description of the performance of such sandwich panels and characteristics of different core materials, see sandwich panels, p. 85.

Moulds

Although GRC being a moulded material offers the architect great flexibility in shapes and contours to be designed, in practice the types of mould and methods of spraying may restrict the size and shape of the unit. This is particularly true for sandwich panels. As with GRP, the effect of the mould costs on the finished panel are dependent upon complexity, numbers taken off the mould and the

Fig. 3.3   Manual spraying of GRC (courtesy of GRC Ltd).

number of specials required. It is necessary, therefore, to keep the number of specials to a minimum. Where possible the basic mould should be adaptable to produce panel variants. For example, at the UOP Fragrances factory, Tadworth, Surrey (architects: Piano and Rogers), various adaptor pieces were inserted in the timber and marine ply moulds to provide the seven panel variants, and detachable pieces were needed to allow moulding of the complex edge shapes.

Most GRC production using the spray method requires anything up to 24 hours before demoulding. Thus the speed of production will be determined by the number of moulds available. Requirements for higher mould utilisation have led to developments in rapid-setting types of Portland cement and accelerated dewatering processes.

The number of units to be cast will determine the material from which the mould is made. In general, timber moulds are used for 'short' runs where a small number of units are required (approx. thirty castings can be obtained from a single mould). For most purposes, moulds in GRP are the most appropriate material as they are more durable than timber and offer a better standard of surface finish. Steel moulds can be used for long continuous runs.

Using spray production the designer should be aware that it is possible to obtain a smooth finish only on the mould side. The non-moulded face will have the textured surface of the compaction roller or a trowelled finish. There are a few exceptions to this; for example, using a floated cement and sand finish or where sophisticated high throughput standard production lines are used (e.g. for PVC coated standard insulated panels produced by Fenox (UK) Ltd, and their Dutch parent company Veldhoen Isolatic BV, Holland), where two skins are bonded under pressure to a structural foam core. Such techniques cannot be used for one-off applications in cladding.

Finishes

Normally GRC components would cure to the greyish colour of ordinary Portland cement. White Portland cement has often been used for cladding panels to improve their appearance, but complete uniformity of colour from one panel to another may not be achievable because of variations during manufacture. Panels produced in smooth surfaced moulds will have a glossy finish on one side only, which tends to accentuate small surface defects and show up the inherent post-curing patchiness of the material. The cement-rich layer at the surface may also show a slight surface crazing. For example, according to Young (1980), panels at the Melrose Centre, Milton Keynes (architects: Colquhoun and Miller), showed that a combination of white cement, a smooth glossy mould surface and the inherent post-curing patchiness of the material and slight surface crazing produce an effect not unlike marble.

There are three basic ways in which the colour and texture of GRC can be modified:

1. Surface treatments and textured moulds.
2. Pigmented colouring.
3. Applied paint coatings.

Surface treatments and textured moulds

As with concrete, some surface treatments can be applied either during moulding using textured moulds or after casting using acid-etched, grit blasting or smooth grinding techniques. These techniques can be particularly valuable in removing any excess cement/sand laitance, and hence reduce tendency of crazing. Considerable skill is needed in retaining minimum component thickness after the treatment has been applied. Any textured layers must be considered as surface treatment only and not taken into account in determining the design of the cladding.

Large aggregate finishes, as used with precast concrete, are not normally recommended, as these require to be embedded in 10–15 mm of cement, making the panels heavier and less manœuvrable. Normally only aggregate less than 12 mm is used because of the excessive amount of GRC required behind larger aggregate. An interesting recent development is the proprietary panel system by Fenox (UK) Ltd, which includes a PVC plastisol finish produced by spraying GRC on to a PVC film 1200 mm wide in a continuous production line.

Pigmented colouring

As with asbestos cement, pre-pigmented cements are available in subdued colours; however, glass fibres in the material tend to show up when using darker-pigmented colours and there are problems of colour match from panel to panel.

Applied paint coatings

As with all cement-based systems, GRC is also subject to moisture movement in that it expands during water uptake and contracts when drying. Great care should therefore be taken in the consideration of any applied coating. Impermeable coatings for external use should generally be avoided, as they can lead to an increased risk of interstitial condensation, particularly with sandwich panels. If the panels are not allowed to 'breathe', then moisture migrating to the surface will cause any impermeable paint to blister or flake.

Proprietary textured permeable finishes, such as those used for coating external masonry, e.g. Muroplast, Sandtex and Glamrock are often used. Such finishes were used at Heathrow Eurolounge and at Newton Heath Library (see Fig. 3.4).

Clear surface coatings of the silicone type, which are particularly useful in protecting the surface of white GRC panels against dirt and fingermarks, can be used without fear of blistering, as they allow the GRC to breathe.

Fig. 3.4   Newton Heath Library (courtesy of GRC Ltd).

Care must be taken in applying paint coatings, whether in the factory or on-site, in ensuring that the surface is free from grease or any trace of mould release agent so that an adequate bond is maintained between the GRC and the paint system base coat.

Performance characteristics

Wind loading

Simplified tables are now available for determining spanning characteristics of varying thickness of GRC in relation to wind loading (see Table 3.1). For example, 10–12 mm flat sheets will span 1.0 m under a wind pressure of 1.0 N/m², but sheet of the same thickness can be profiled or ribbed to span up to 4.0 m under the same wind pressure. For greater spans or wind pressure, it may be necessary to design using sandwich construction.

Thermal characteristics

A 20 mm single-skin GRC construction of approximate density 1800–2100 kg/m³ gives a negligible insulation value, being in the region of 5.0 W/m² °C. For improved thermal insulation (up to a *U* value of 0.7 W/m² °C), it is necessary to incorporate an insulation core into the construction or to incorporate some

Table 3.1   Panel thickness and span (courtesy Fibreglass Ltd) The following tables give a guide to the recommended panel thicknesses for different panel types.

Single-skin flat sheet

Panel span (m)	Minimum required GRC thickness (mm)		
	0.5 kN/m² Wind pressure	*1.0 kN/m²* Wind pressure	*1.5 kN/m²* Wind pressure
0.5	4	6	7
1.0	8	11	14
1.5	12	17	
2.0	16		

Profiled single skin (10 mm thick)

For a profiled single-skin panel the table below should be used to select the panel design type based on the required span and wind pressure.

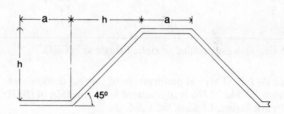

Panel span (m)	Wind pressure 0.5 kN/m² h(mm) × a (mm)	Wind pressure 1.0 kN/m² h (mm) × a (mm)	Wind pressure 1.5 kN/m² h (mm) × a (mm)
1.0	50 × 100	50 × 100	50 × 100
1.5	50 × 100	50 × 100	50 × 100
2.0	50 × 100	100 × 150	100 × 150
2.5	100 × 150	100 × 150	150 × 200
3.0	100 × 150	150 × 200	200 × 300
3.5	150 × 200	200 × 300	200 × 300
4.0	200 × 300	200 × 300	Use sandwich panel

Sandwich construction

In selecting parameters for sandwich construction panels, it should be noted that the panel thickness includes two 10 mm thick GRC skins.

Table 3.1 (cont'd.)

Panel span (m)	Minimum recommended overall panel thickness (mm)		
	Wind pressure 0.5 kN/m²	Wind pressure 1.0 kN/m²	Wind pressure 1.5 kN/m²
2.0*	50	50	50
2.5*	65	65	65
3.0*	70	70	75
3.5*	80	80	95
4.0*	95	95	120
4.5	105	105	145
5.0	115	125	175
5.5	140	145	210
6.0	150	170	215

* Can also use profiled or ribbed single skin GRC.

Table 3.2 Thermal performance of varying thickness of GRC sandwich panels. Material from BS 5427:1976 is reproduced by permission of the British Standards Institution, 2 Park Street, London WIA 2bS

			'U' value W/m² °C
	GRC 20 mm		5.0
70 mm	GRC 10 mm PBAC 50 mm GRC 10 mm		2.0
110 mm	GRC 10 mm PBAC 100 mm GRC 10 mm		1.3
100 mm	GRC 10 mm PBAC 30 mm Polystyrene 20 mm PBAC 30 mm GRC 10 mm		0.9
150 mm	GRC 10 mm PBAC 50 mm Polystyrene 30 mm PBAC 50 mm GRC 10 mm		0.7

form of insulation behind a single-skin façade, a method which is finding increasing use in Europe. Table 3.2 shows thermal performance of varying thicknesses of GRC sandwich panels.

Fire performance

The test for fire resistance of a given structure is defined by its performance to BS 476, Part 8:1972. This test has three criteria:

1. Stability: the structure under test must not collapse.
2. Integrity: flames must not penetrate the structure.
3. Insulation: the temperature on the protected side must not rise by an average of more than 140 °C above the initial temperature.

A single skin of GRC will not satisfy the insulation criterion and the standard cement/sand matrix may not maintain integrity. To guarantee integrity in single-skin form it is advisable to use a cement/pulverised fuel ash (PFA) air entrainment mix. This is only used for internal applications at present because of weathering of air-entrained material. A single skin of GRC can provide up to 1 hour fire resistance on all three criteria if a suitable insulant such as 20 mm Mandolite P.20 is applied to the GRC. It is claimed that sandwich construction incorporating 50 mm polystyrene bead aggregate cement can achieve 2 hours' fire resistance in one layer and 4 hours' fire resistance in two layers. As this is for the panel itself, it must be remembered that BS 476 Part 8 applies to the whole construction under test and in the case of panels the jointing and fixing points must also be considered and tested. Fire resistance of various types of single skin and sandwich construction are given in Table 3.3

Glassfibre reinforced cement is non-combustible and is not easily ignitable to BS 476 Part 5, while even with a suitable organic paint finish GRC still complies with the Class O requirements for the fire propagation test BS 476 Part 6.

Acoustic performance

A 10 mm single skin of GRC at 20 kg/m² density gives sound reduction indices from 22 dB at 350 Hz to 39 dB at 4000 Hz, or an average of 30 dB over the normal range of frequencies. Even if the single skin is increased to 20 mm, which is beyond that thickness normally recommended, the average reduction indices will only increase to 35 dB. For greater acoustic performance it is possible to specify sandwich construction; however, if it is necessary to connect the outer and inner skins for structural reasons, this will reduce the sound insulation for the whole panel.

Density

A piece of flat GRC 8 mm thick weighs approximately 16 kg/m². A sandwich panel with two 10 mm skins on a 75 mm polystyrene bead aggregate concrete

Table 3.3 Relationship between wall construction and performance requirement (courtesy Pilkington Ltd)

Wall Construction		Maximum recommended span (1.0 kN/m² wind pressure)	Fire resistance BS 476 Part 8	Weight (approximate)
Single skin		Metres	Hours	kg/m²
	Flat GRC 8 mm thick	0.8	None claimed	16
	Flat GRC 12 mm thick	1.1	None claimed	24
	Profiled or ribbed GRC + 50 mm fibreglass insulation + plasterboard	Up to 4	½	40
	Profiled or ribbed GRC + 50 mm fibreglass insulation + 100 mm concrete block	Up to 4	4	100

Increased depth of profile and stiffening ribs increases the spanning capability of the panel

Sandwich construction				
	10 mm GRC 50 mm PBAC 10 mm GRC	3.0	2	60
Overall panel thickness 70 mm				
	10 mm GRC 60 mm polystyrene 10 mm GRC	3.5	None claimed	42
Overall panel thickness 80 mm				
	10 mm GRC 50 mm PBAC 30 mm polystyrene 50 mm PBAC 10 mm GRC	5.5	4	150
Overall panel thickness 150 mm				

Note: PBAC – polystyrene bead aggregate concrete.

core weighs about 70 kg/m² which is less than 20 per cent of the weight of a precast concrete panel.

Shrinkage and moisture movement

Like other cement-based materials, GRC exhibits non-reversible shrinkage during the curing process and long-term moisture movement caused by changes in humidity. The incorporation of 25 per cent silica sand into the matrix reduces both types of shrinkage but, even so, actual movements in use could in theory be 1.5 mm/m. In practice movements of 1.0 mm/m may be experienced, which is approximately double that of ordinary reinforced concrete. Care has to be taken in the design of fixings to allow for this movement (see Figs. 3.10 and 3.11).

Sandwich panels

The choice of the type of construction, single skin, profiled or sandwich construction, will be governed by a combination of requirements: fire, thermal, acoustic, weight, etc. that need to be satisfied. Table 3.3 shows the relationship between various types of wall construction and the performance requirements for spans, fire resistance and weight, which are usually the most critical.

The total effective depth of large panels can usually be reduced using sandwich construction, as large single-skin panels would require deep stiffening ribs to prevent deflection under load.

In sandwich construction a larger overall thickness than indicated by strength calculations would usually be used to satisfy fire and thermal characteristics and also minimise bowing. This may also be minimised by limiting panel length or width, since the effect is proportional to the square of either dimension; increased panel thickness has a directly beneficial effect in minimising bowing. Bowing has not been a problem in single-skin construction with separate insulation applied on-site.

If the panel is required to act as a true sandwich and for the core to have sufficient shear strength, the need to form a good bond between the GRC and the insulating core is important to prevent delamination of the core from the skin which may be caused, in turn, through bowing of the panel.

Sandwich panels have tended to predominate in the UK. For example, RACS Superstore, Thanet, Kent (architects: Royal Arsenal Co-operative Society Ltd), is clad with what are claimed to be the largest GRC panels manufactured in Europe to date. These panels weigh just over 4 t and have thermal insulation of 0.9 W/m² °C. In recent overseas contracts, however, this requirement for thermal insulation and other performance requirements have been achieved using single-skin construction, ribbed where necessary, with separate insulation applied on-site. For example, the Sports and Leisure Centre in Saudi Arabia (architects/consulting engineers: Slater Hodder/Cooper McDonald), uses GRC on the fascia panels to the roof and barrel vaults. This move away from sandwich panels is partly due to the greater thermal stresses and hence bowing problems in hot countries and partly due to manufacturing difficulties.

Bridging webs used to give stiffness to larger panels can cause ghosting of the surface finish, such as that reported by Young (1978) at the UOP Fragrances factory where, although a special case using a site-applied urethane paint finish, the egg crate construction could be seen on the panel face. Young suggests the most probable explanation is that paint on the insulated skins (130 mm polystyrene) cured at a different rate to that in those areas where webs linked skins and at the edges of window surrounds. However, he also reports (1980) feedback from the Melrose Centre, Milton Keynes, where 77 mm polystyrene core was used with two skins of 6 mm GRC and no ghosting of stiffening webs occurred. He suggests that this may be because the panels were left as white Portland cement on all surfaces and that the method of production meant that the insulation was not added until about 2 hours after spraying. The decision to use the non-moulded finish on the outside of the panels may account for the same lack of apparent ghosting on the panels at the Scicon Computer Centre, where 50 mm polystyrene core was used.

Polystyrene bead aggregate concrete is an important core material because it avoids the need for the concrete stiffening webs, thus reducing cold bridging. Unlike the expanded plastics, which are produced as preformed flat slabs, polystyrene bead aggregate concrete is supplied as a wet mix and can therefore fill complex mould profiles with ease. Since the complete sandwich is constructed in the wet state, adhesion between skins and core occurs on curing. It also has excellent fire resistance properties, although its thermal insulation properties are not so good as polystyrene foam. Its only disadvantage is the time it takes for the panel core to dry out and any possible risk of shrinkage of the GRC outer skins.

In order to improve the thermal performance of the panel and, at the same time, improve its fire resistance and stiffness characteristics, multiple sandwich panels of GRC, PBAC and rigid polystyrene foam have been used (see Table 3.2).

Long-term performance

As some of the properties of GRC, particularly tensile and impact strength, diminish with time, it has been necessary to establish the extent of these changes. Extensive natural exposure trials have been carried out by BRE and Pilkington, both at UK and overseas sites. Research on predicting property change by accelerated test procedure has also been carried out and this has been reported on in the journal of *Cement and Concrete Research* (Litherland *et al.*, 1981).

These ageing characteristics of GRC have always been recognised and the design methods and design stress levels recommended for use have always made allowance for the changes that occur. These have been based on estimates of long-term properties which can be regarded as minimum values over the lifetime of the component.

Pilkington has promoted, and continues to advocate, a conservative approach to GRC design in order to avoid component failures in the early uses of the material. Because of this there have been no cases of serious failure of the material since it was introduced.

The long-term properties of GRC are discussed in BRE Digest No. 216 (BRE, 1978). This includes Table 1 showing the strength properties of spray-dewatered ordinary Portland cement GRC for 1, 5 and 20 years. After 20 years the tensile strength is estimated to fall from a mean 15.5 MN/m^2 to 7 MN/m^2 and the impact strength from 24 MN/m^2 to 4 MN/m^2. The Digest states that temperature and humidity both have a marked effect on the rate of loss of strength of air-stored GRC. At high temperature (50 °C) and high humidity (90% RH) the initial rapid decrease in strength occurs within about 30 days. Proctor (1980) showed in a paper to the Concrete International Symposium how bending strengths of dewatered GRC in UK weather falls over 20 years from approx. 37 MN/m^2 to 15 MN/m^2. At the same time the Building Research Establishment (1979) published the results of their 10-year tests on the properties of GRC in November 1979 (see BRE IP36/79 – Table 2) which confirmed and supported the recommendation set out in Digest 216 and gave revised estimated mean strength properties of spray-dewatered OPC/GRC after 20 years. While these tests were carried out on a matrix not typical of that used commercially and for a spray-dewatered composite which is not in common use for cladding, even so, they can be taken as indicative that the tensile and impact strength of GRC will fall below their original values in a predictable manner over a period of time. The designer (engineer) therefore has to select a working stress level in design that will give a reasonable margin of safety with the passage of time. Pilkington Bros. (1979), in their design guide (Section 4) suggest that the safety margins should be decided upon for a particular circumstance in consultation with the architect. *For most applications a design stress of 6.0 MN/m^2 for bending and 3.0 MN/m^2 for direct tension is recommended.*

Using the above approach it has been found that the margin between failure and the design conditions is at least five times when newly made. This may fall over the life of a component to two to three times, which will still leave an adequate margin of safety.

Developments in improving the long-term durability of GRC have led to Pilkington's subsidiary, Fibreglass Ltd, introducing an improved alkali-resistant fibre, Cem-fil 2, which greatly extends the strength and toughness retention of GRC products. They claim at least fivefold increase in retention of strain capacity, and a three to four times extension of tensile strength retention over the working life of a component.

Jointing

The techniques used to seal joints in GRC components or panels are similar to those used for precast concrete or GRP. There are essentially four main ways of dealing with joints (see Fig. 3.5). These are by using:

1. Gaskets;
2. The use of baffles in an open-drained joint;
3. Using face sealants; or
4. The use of cover strips.

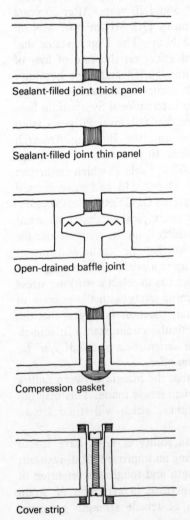

Sealant-filled joint thick panel

Sealant-filled joint thin panel

Open-drained baffle joint

Compression gasket

Cover strip

Fig. 3.5 Types of joints between GRC panels.

Gasket joints

Gaskets are only effective where positive pressure is available to deform or compress them. The Fenox (UK) Ltd, patent joint, for example (see Fig. 3.6), incorporates a top-hat section with captive nut to pull back a metal cover strip against a neoprene gasket. Advantage can be taken of the quality of the edge profile, which is normally possible in GRC, to use push-in fir-cone gaskets, as used, for example, at the UOP Fragrances factory (architects: Piano and Rogers) (see Fig. 3.7). These gaskets incorporate barbed legs which can be pushed into position in the joint. One problem using such gaskets is that the moulded GRC nibs to receive the gasket have only one mould face, and however well the back face is compacted, minor variations in thickness will occur, which can cause

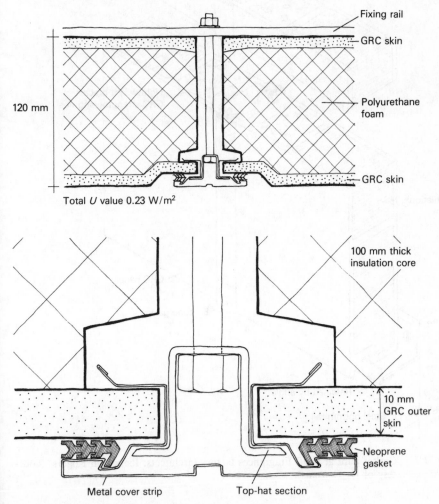

Fig. 3.6 Fenox (UK) Ltd, patent joint.

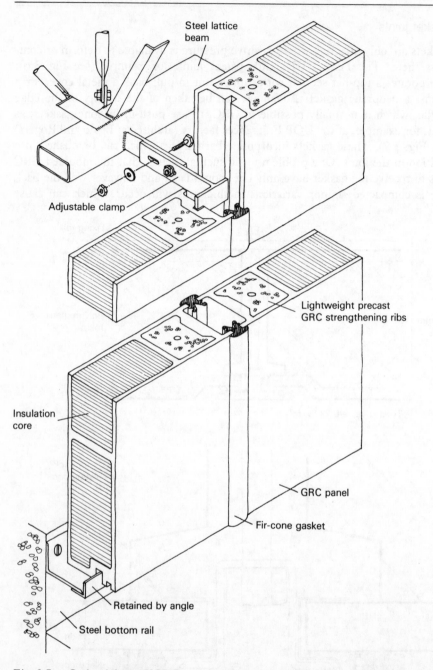

Fig. 3.7 Gasket joint at UOP Fragrances factory (architects: Piano and Rogers) (courtesy of D. Cousans).

points of weakness for an effective weatherproof seal. These nibs can be wrapped in tape to take up any tolerances in surface defects as a result of manufacture in order to gain a tight fit before applying the compression gasket. The UOP Fragrances factory also uses a push-in gasket on the inside face; some difficulty may be experienced in sealing past the adjustable clamps in such a detail.

Another problem with gasket joints is that they depend upon extremely tight tolerances in joint size and may only really work in conjunction with a system of adjustable fixing devices. Typical permissible joint range clearances are 5–10 mm. The use of slotted holes and T-clamps at UOP Fragrances resulted in precise location of panels, allowing the use of this method of gasket jointing even at the corner detail. Direct glazing of windows into GRC is also possible using neoprene gaskets.

Open-drained joints

One of the requirements of an open-drained joint is the baffle groove deep enough to accommodate the baffle at the maximum and minimum joint ranges. Typical baffle groove depths are 30 mm. Such deep grooves are difficult to form during GRC manufacture. Further, it is not always easy to fix the baffle strip at the head of the joint. For these reasons this form of joint is not often used for GRC panels.

Mastic sealants

Various mastic sealants, including polysulphides, polyurethane and silicone rubbers have been used, but their success depends upon good surface preparation and the use of correct primers. The sealant surface may be exposed to ultraviolet light and its long-term characteristics are therefore questionable. Manufacturers' recommendations for sealants must be closely followed at all times. Sealants designed to bond to smooth surfaces should be specified and care taken to ensure that any silicone face sealer to the panel is not carried round the edges of the panel, as this inhibits adhesion of the sealant.

Where a back-up strip or gasket acting as a secondary seal is required, this can be retained within a groove as the small depth of groove can be formed in GRC without difficulty.

Cover strips

Although in theory it is possible to disguise the joint using a cover strip, these are not often used, partly because they are not normally visually acceptable and partly because of the design of the intersection between vertical and horizontal cover strips it is almost impossible to maintain weather tightness.

Fixings

Fixing methods using angle cleats and dowel fixings are similar to those used for precast concrete. Glassfibre reinforced cement panels are best supported at the base and restrained at the top; intermediate fixings should be avoided. Typical fixings for fixing panels back to their supporting framework are shown in Fig. 3.8.

It is most important that allowances be made for the thermal, moisture and any structural movements of the GRC which are approximately double those of precast concrete. For cladding panels these provisions for movement are usually

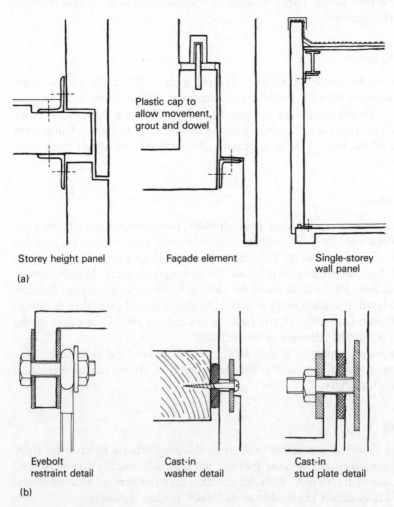

Plastic cap to
allow movement,
grout and dowel

Storey height panel

(a)

Façade element

Single-storey
wall panel

Eyebolt
restraint detail

(b)

Cast-in
washer detail

Cast-in
stud plate detail

Fig. 3.8   Typical fixings using GRC: (a) sandwich construction fixings; (b) single-skin fixings.

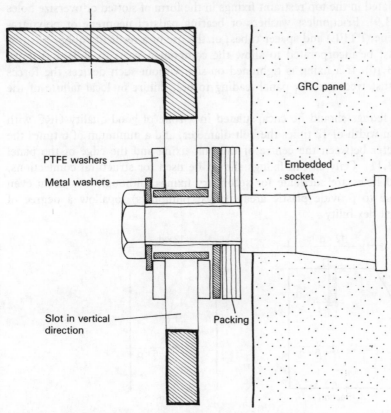

Fig. 3.9   Slotted fixings to allow movement at top of panel.

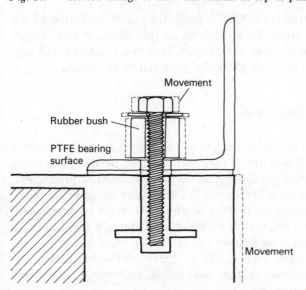

Fig. 3.10   Resilient rubber bush fixing to allow movement.

accommodated in the top restraint fixings in the form of slotted or oversize holes (see Fig. 3.9). Frictionless washers or bearing pads of neoprene or polytetrafluorethylene (PTFE) and spacer tubes, or the use of a resilient rubber bush or spring must be incorporated to allow the component parts to slide and move (see Fig. 3.10). If a fixing is tightened on-site without such devices the forces will be transferred into the panel leading to bolt failure or local failure of the GRC.

Cast-in fixings should be encapsulated in a zone of good-quality GRC with a minimum width of 12 times the bolt diameter, and a minimum of 6 times the bolt diameter between the centre of the bolt fixing and the edge of the panel (see Fig. 3.11). Only cast-in fixings should be used for structural connections. Site-drilled holes are adequate for secondary fixings, although it is usual even in this case to provide plastic area fixings (philiplugs) to allow a degree of dimensional flexibility.

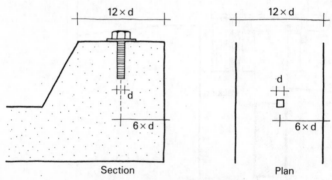

Fig. 3.11 Minimum cover to cast-in fixings.

Where single-skin construction in GRC is used, the panels can be fixed back to the secondary framing using cleats mounted on the stiffening ribs. Figure 3.12 shows a typical example where the panel is fixed to a horizontal rail supported by steel uprights at intervals along the perimeter of the façade.

Panel dimensions and tolerances

Although in theory there is no real restriction on the length of panel, in practice this is normally limited to 4–6 m due to problems of lifting, handling and fixing of units. Maximum widths of panels depend upon the method of production. For manual spraying this is normally limited to 2 m. Where windows are incorporated within a panel, a minimum mullion width of 200 mm is recommended. Glassfibre reinforced cement single-skin thickness is minimum 6 mm and maximum of 18 mm for sprayed material (see Fig. 3.13). For premix material the minimum thickness is normally 10 mm with no upper limit within reason.

Tolerances in panels are similar to those used for precast concrete, but should not exceed ± 3 mm for small panels.

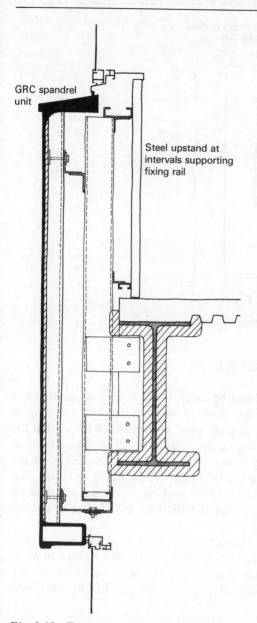

GRC spandrel unit

Steel upstand at intervals supporting fixing rail

Fig. 3.12 Example of single-skin GRC spandrel panel detail.

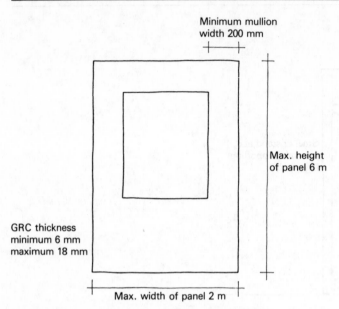

Minimum mullion
width 200 mm

Max. height
of panel 6 m

GRC thickness
minimum 6 mm
maximum 18 mm

Max. width of panel 2 m

Fig. 3.13 Typical panel dimensions and tolerances.

Handling of units on-site and storage

Because of the ease in which GRC can be formed in a variety of shapes, it is not uncommon to avoid the potentially troublesome eaves detail by cranking or curving the panels at their junction with the roof. Such panels were used at the fire station at the National Exhibition Centre (see Fig. 3.15) and at Heathrow Eurolounge. Special equipment may be necessary for handling such units on-site and care must be taken in designing the fixing devices for lifting to ensure that these do not show on the outside face. Highly profiled panels are also difficult to store and transport, and cranked panels will twist and distort if stacked unsupported on edge (see Fig. 3.14).

Also large upstands and long unsupported ends tend to settle when in their 'green' state and care must be taken during manufacture and storage to avoid sagging of unsupported ends. If this is not done, problems can occur in controlling the size of joints between panels due to difficulties in ensuring alignment of panels during erection.

Repair on-site

Although it is possible for specialist contractors to repair minor defects on-site using manually applied cement/sand slurry where structural damage has taken place in the form of large holes and the fibre/cement bond has been broken

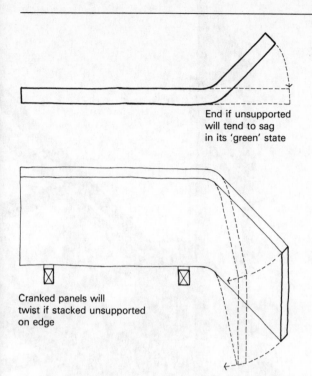

End if unsupported
will tend to sag
in its 'green' state

Cranked panels will
twist if stacked unsupported
on edge

Fig. 3.14 Cranked panels need supporting to avoid distrortion.

down, panels should be removed and returned to the factory for repair under closer quality workmanship control, or preferably replaced by a new panel. Panels with surface texture treatments should be resprayed to avoid any patchiness occurring on the panel face where the repair has taken place.

References

Brookes, A. J. and Ward, M. A. (1981) *'The art of construction – GRC claddings'*, Architects' Journal, 15.7.1981.

Building Research Establishment (1974) 'Glass fibre reinforced cement', BRE Current Paper, CP 79/74, Aug. 1974.

Building Research Establishment (1976) 'A study of the properties of Cem-fil OPC composites', BRE Current Paper, CP 38/76, June 1976.

Building Research Establishment (1978) 'GRC', Digest No. 216, Aug. 1978; HMSO.

Building Research Establishment (1979) 'Properties of GRC: ten-year results', BRE Internal Paper, IP 36/79.

Glassfibre Reinforced Cement Association (1980) 'The Developing Success of GRC', *Proceedings of the International Congress on Glassfibre Reinforced Cement* (London 10–12 Oct. 1979). GRCA: London.

Litherland, K. L., Oakley, D. R. and Proctor, B. A. (1980) 'The use of accelerated age-

ing procedures to predict the long-term strength of GRC composites', *Cement and Concrete Research*, vol. II, No. 3, 1981, 455–66.

Pilkington Bros. PLC (1979) *Cem-fil GRC. Design Guide*, 2nd edn, Jan. 1979, Pilkington Bros. Ltd, St Helens, Merseyside.

Proctor, B. A. (1980) 'Properties and performance of GRC', *Proceedings of Fibrous Concrete Symposium 1980*, Concrete Society: London, pp. 69–86.

Young, J. (1978) 'GRC – a briefing guide to architects', *Architects' Journal*, 15.2.1978; 8.3.1978; 29.3.1978; 19.4.1978.

Young, J. (1980) *Designing with GRC*, Architectural Press: London.

Fig. 3.15 Lifting GRC panels on-site (National Exhibition Centre) (courtesy of GRC Ltd).

Chapter 4

Profiled metal and asbestos cement cladding

Introduction

In recent years there has been an increase in the use of profiled sheet not only for industrial buildings and farm buildings, but also, with the development of more sophisticated finishes and the introduction of a wider variety of trapezoidal profiles, for other types of buildings such as schools, offices and even hospitals (eg. use of horizontal profiled cladding for the Oxford Regional Health Authority system). Manufacturers have been aware of the need to introduce new types of profiles and ranges of colours, offering a more attractive appearance than that provided by traditional corrugated sheeting. Architects have attempted to use the materials in innovative ways with sheets laid horizontally or at an angle. The introduction of curved sheets, such as 'Floclad' by Ash and Lacey (Lyall, 1981), has also helped to promote profiled cladding for uses other than industrial buildings.

The cost of profiled claddings also compares favourably with other materials when one considers the total cost of whole assembly including secondary framework. A rough guide to types of lightweight cladding, taking a base price factor of 10 for profiled aluminium, is as follows:

	Relative costs
Asbestos cement profiled sheet and secondary framing	8
Steel profiled sheet and secondary framing	9
Aluminium profiled sheet and secondary framing	10
GRP panels profiled sheet and secondary framing	16
Curtain walling incorporating single-skin panels	25
Sheet metal insulated panel construction	40

Recent legislation of thermal requirements has led to the frequent specification for industrial purposes of 'composite' panels of profiled metal with bonded insulating materials and most manufacturers of profiled sheeting will also now offer these 'composite' varieties. Although these are more expensive in material cost than conventional profiled sheeting with *in situ*, site-applied, insulation, they do have the advantage of quicker erection and also the spans of secondary

Table 4.1 Key characteristics to consider when selecting asbestos cement, steel or aluminium cladding

	Asbestos cement	Steel	Aluminium
Appearance			
Texture	Self-textured but a smooth epoxy finish can be applied	Grained or smooth	Stucco, grained or smooth
Colour	Limited range, generally dark colours	Large range, including bright colours	
Profiles	Rounded	Round or sharp	Round or sharp
Finish	Natural finish, integral colour or factory-applied paint	Needs applied finish to resist corrosion	Applied finish not necessary but coating usually applied to increase durability and reduce glare
Strength and stability	Bending strength varies with form of profile	Good tensile strength and impact resistance	Less resistant than steel to soft impact
Size	Restricted lengths (3.05 m) and requires cladding rails at closer centres. Maximum width 1.2 m	Maximum length is unlimited: preferred maximum lengths 13 m. Maximum width 1.0 m	Maximum length is unlimited: preferred maximum 13 m. Maximum width 1.00 m
Compatibility	No reaction with cement concrete or plaster. Check with manufacturer for compatibility with aluminium	Hot-dip coated steel requires caution in detailing	Needs to be isolated from some building materials e.g. steel cladding rails and cement
Costs	As a rule, asbestos cement has tended to be cheaper than steel which is cheaper than aluminium. However, this applies only to the basic cladding material as final costs may be affected by finishes chosen and costs of the supporting structure		
Other characteristics	The comparative performance of these materials with regard to fire, durability, thermal and working characteristics, is not a primary factor in deciding which of the three is most suitable for a particular task		
Composite claddings	Composite claddings are only available in steel and aluminium		

framing can be increased, taking advantage of the composite structural performance of the sheet and its integral insulation core.

Table 4.1 shows key characteristics to consider when selecting asbestos
cement, steel or aluminium cladding. Due to problems of fire resistance, low
resistance to impact and general appearance (rounded profiles and available
finishes), the use of asbestos cement tends to be limited to roof cladding in industrial buildings; Habitat warehouse in Wallingford, see Fig. 4.1 (architects:

Fig. 4.1   Habitat warehouse, Wallingford (architects Ahrends, Burton and Koralek).

Fig. 4.2   IBM Greenford (architects Foster Associates) (courtesy of Plannja Dobel
Ltd).

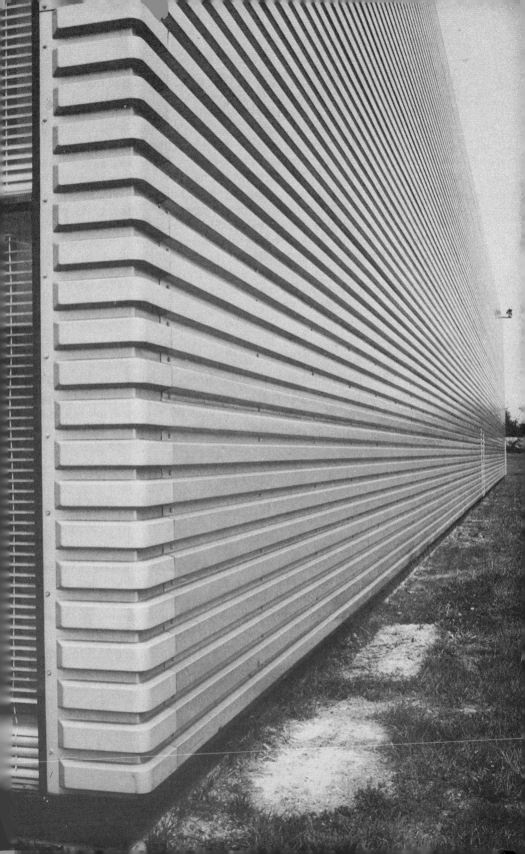

Ahrends Burton and Koralek), might be seen as an exception to that. Both steel and aluminium offer a wide variety of sharper (trapezoidal) profiles and coloured finishes and can be used horizontally or vertically with patent bending processes available for specially formed corner junctions. The use of horizontal metal sheeting at the IBM offices at Greenford (see Fig 4.2; architects: Foster Associates), for example, has encouraged other architects to use profiled metal sheeting in a similar manner. The selection of either steel or aluminium may be a personal choice. Aluminium is nominally more expensive but, on the other hand, is lighter and, therefore, in theory, needs less framing. In practice, because the actual difference is 1.5 kg/m², this makes no difference to the framing in most cases. Maybe the specifier is influenced by steel being, in theory, more susceptible to rusting at the edges of the sheets. In truth, the choice probably rests on the types of finishes available or even the standard of technical back-up service provided by the manufacturers.

Definitions

Constrado (1980) on profiled steel cladding defines 'cladding' as:

> The external envelope of the building which normally carries no loading beyond its own weight plus the loads imposed by snow, wind and during maintenance. It is the term used when the steel sheet (coated or uncoated) is exposed to the elements. Cladding for walls is sometimes known as walling or siding and cladding for roofs is generally known as roof sheeting or roof cladding.

and 'roof decking' as:

> The part of the envelope, on the roof, which supports insulation and waterproofing plus its own weight, plus imposed loads resulting from snow, wind, maintenance and sometimes access. The steel sheet usually forms the inner layer and is not exposed to the elements, unlike roof cladding.

For the purpose of this chapter, we shall now be discussing wall cladding in asbestos cement, steel and aluminium profiled sheets. Profiled steel and aluminium sheets are available in sinusoidal, symmetrical and asymmetrical trapezoidal profiles. According to the PSA Method of Building Guide (1979), these can be defined (see Fig. 4.3) as:

1. Sinusoidal – where crests and troughs are symmetrical and have the shape of a sine curve.
2. Symmetrical trapezoidal – where crests and troughs are the same width and the sloping sections are at a constant angle.
3. Asymmetrical trapezoidal – crests and troughs are unequal in width. The section can be used with either surface outside provided the organic coating is on the correct side.

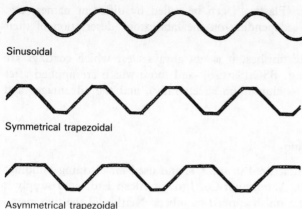

Sinusoidal

Symmetrical trapezoidal

Asymmetrical trapezoidal

Fig. 4.3   Terminology of profiles.

The industry

Steel profiled cladding

Coiled steel sheet is only manufactured in the UK by the British Steel Corporation (BSC), who supply it in three main versions:

1. Organic coated on a galvanised substrate as in 'Colourcoat' and 'Stelvetite'.
2. Galvanised only to BS 2989 for 3 in corrugated sheets to BS 3083: 1980.
3. Undercoated (black steel) to BS 1449 for others to apply their own metallic or organic coatings.

Although BSC profiles have their own fabricating works at Ayecliffe, Darlington, in most cases they supply the coiled sheet for rolling into profiles by other manufacturers. Most manufacturers sell their rolled products to specialist fixing contractors. Only two operators, H. H. Robertson (UK) Ltd, and Briggs Amasco, have their own erection teams and can therefore offer the combined supply and erection services for profiled sheeting. Of these only H. H. Robertson offers a total service embracing all aspects of organic coating, profiling, supply and erection.

Some manufacturers claim to roll profiles of steel, taking advantage of modern steel processing methods, to attain a higher yield strength of 320–550 N/mm^2. However, high-tensile steels do not reduce deflection for any given profile or loading and therefore the spans cannot be increased for deflection-controlled sheets. Thus if deflection is the criteria then high-tensile steel offers no real advantage, but if strength is the criteria then spans can be increased.

Although in the UK the coiled steel with its factory-applied finish mainly comes from one source, namely BSC, it can sometimes be confusing to the specifier that the same finish, e.g. 'Plastisol', can be called by different names, e.g. 'Colourclad' or 'Everclad', depending on the fabricators' description of their particular product range.

Similarly in considering finishes, it is not always clear which coatings are applied before forming (e.g. BSC Plastisol) and those which are applied after forming (e.g. Bacocolour – aluminium sheets only), and the advantages and disadvantages of each.

Aluminium profiled cladding

All aluminium sheet manufactured in the UK and used for cladding buildings is produced by the British Aluminium Co. Ltd, or Alcan Ltd, who supply it finished, or plain, to have a finish applied by others. Neither of the two manufacturers will supply and erect their own material, but there are a number of fabricators of profiled metal, such as Precision Metal Forming, or E. R. Dyer (Manchester), who will offer an erection service.

In other countries, mainly Sweden, it is possible to produce aluminium by other methods of production such as continuous cast coil, and in this way some foreign manufacturers (e.g. Granges Essem) claim that they can produce alloys of greater tensile strength and therefore, for the same span, reduce the thickness (and thus cost) of their material. However, as with steel, these materials are likely to be more expensive than the UK-based product.

Asbestos cement profiled cladding

The four main suppliers of profiled asbestos cement sheeting in the UK, Eternit Building Products Ltd, Cape Universal Cladding Ltd, TAC Construction Materials Ltd and Tunnel Building Products Ltd, all produce profiles according to the profile classes listed in BS 690 (sinusoidal only).

Profiles

Profiled asbestos cement cladding sheets are available in sinusoidal or asymmetrical trapezoidal profiles of profile depths 15–30 mm (e.g. standard 3), 30–50 mm (e.g. standard 6), 50–90 mm (e.g. double six) and 45–50·mm (e.g. panel sheet).

Profiled aluminium sheets to BS 4868 are produced in depths of 8–38 mm and 38–50 mm; however, there are many more trapezoidal profiles produced between 8 mm and 90 mm profile depth, as illustrated in the manufacturers' catalogues. For a complete table of all profiles, see PSA Method of Building (1979).

Profiled steel sheets are available up to about 13 m long with cover widths up to 100 mm. Trapezoidal sections are usually made in lengths to order. Sinusoidal sections are available in stock lengths. The profiles of sinusoidal sections are defined in BS 3083 and CP 143: Part 10.

Sinusoidal profiled steel sheets to BS 3083 are produced in depths of 19 mm. However, there are many more trapezoidal profiles produced up to 100 mm deep, as illustrated in the manufacturers' catalogues. For a complete table of all UK steel profiles, see Constrado publications (1980).

Architects often require a tapering closed profile flashing (see Fig. 4.4) particularly where sheets about window details. These can be produced in asbestos cement and aluminium, but are more difficult in steel. Some steel tapering pieces are available, but they are normally small profiles and may be limited in cover width.

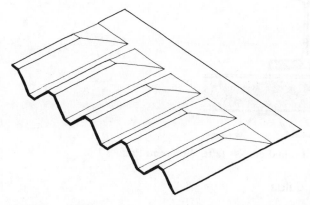

Fig. 4.4   Tapering closed profile flashings available in asbestos cement and aluminium.

Corner flashing details and profiles are also an important consideration. Some curved eaves and round corners are now available in metal to match the main sheeting. See for example European Profiles (Fig. 4.5).

There has also been an increased interest shown by architects in recent years in the curved forms possible in profiled sheets. Trapezoidal aluminium profiles can be fully or partly curved in their length by Alcan or British Aluminium to a minimum radius of 3000 mm. Tighter radii can be produced using crimped profiles such as those developed by Ash and Lacey as Floclad. Initially a process for steel, it has now been licensed to British Aluminium for aluminium profiles. Curved insulation sheets are also now available.

Design guidance

As well as the manufacturers' own design manuals with specific data provided on such factors as loadings, there are a number of publications offering guidance on the specification of profiled cladding. These include:

107

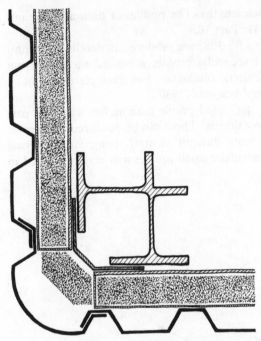

Fig. 4.5   Curved eaves and round corners (after European Profiles Ltd).

PSA Method of Building guide

This includes definitions (p. 36), gives safe temperature ranges and estimates of durability for different finishes. It is intended to help the designer to evaluate the existing manufacturers' products by providing comparative tables of profiles for all types of profiled cladding. It also includes application details (PSA Method of Building, 1979).

CEGB guide

This includes recommendations on construction, weatherproofing, fixings, loadings and strength, appearance, durability and other performance factors (Central Electricity Generating Board, 1970).

Constrado guide

This shows steel profiles available from all UK manufacturers and gives permissible span tables for each. Application details are included and also available colours in Plastisol finishes (p. 18) (Constrado, 1980).

Metal Roof Deck Association

This gives codes of design and technical requirements of roof decking (Metal Roof Deck Association, 1970).

Fig. 4.6 Production of absbestos cement sheets (courtesy of TAC Construction Materials Ltd).

Architects' Journal

This gives drawing board data for all types of profiled sheets, including methods of jointing and fixing sheets with limits of pitch and methods of lapping roof sheets (Brookes, 1980; Falconer, 1981).

British Standard

In addition to the various standards listed later for specific types of cladding and their finishes, BS 5427: 1976 *Code of Practice for performance and loading criteria for profiled sheeting in building*, offers general guidance on all types of profiled sheeting (British Standards, 1976).

In addition, some manufacturers' design manuals provide application details with typical solutions for corner, head and sill details.

Method of manufacture

Asbestos cement

Asbestos is an inorganic material which can be broken down into fibres when milled and used to reinforce thin cement sheets. These sheets are then pressed (not rolled) over templates to form profiled sheets and cured to a consistent mature product (see Fig. 4.6). It is not possible using this mechanical process to produce sheets with sharp arris to the profiles as with steel or aluminium. Coloured finishes can be applied either during manufacture or as a through colour (iron oxide or carbon black pigmentation) or as an applied surface coating. Some problems has been experienced with site coating of asbestos cement.

Metal profiled cladding

In the UK aluminium is produced by the electrolytic reduction of alumina from which two types of alloys are made, principally with magnesium, silicon and manganese. These can be hot and cold rolled to form flat sheets or coils.

Steel is made from iron which is processed with additives such as carbon and manganese to give it added toughness and durability. It is rolled into flat sheets

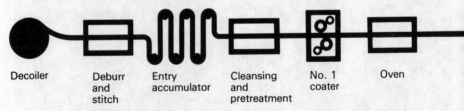

| Decoiler | Deburr and stitch | Entry accumulator | Cleansing and pretreatment | No. 1 coater | Oven |

Fig. 4.7   Typical steel rolling and coating plant (courtesy of H. H. Robertson).

or coils and is usually given a protective zinc coating in a hot dip bath. The sheet may then be profiled or cut for site painting or, more usually, given a liquid or bonded coating before profiling and cutting.

Sheet steel and aluminium coil is supplied to the rolling mill for coating and rolling. A typical coating line for sheet steel would consist of the following parts (see Fig. 4.7):

Galvanising plant

Black steel is de-coiled, continuously cleaned and pretreated prior to zinc coating. A thickness of zinc coating is controlled to the requisite tolerance by means of an air knife, which removes the excess zinc. After galvanising and cooking, the strip is re-coiled.

Coating line

De-coil strip. To maintain continuous operation successive coils are mechanically stitched together. Time to allow this operation to be done is provided by means of an accumulator system at the feed ends of the line.

Pretreatment. Remove oil, grease and surface residues by degreasing and zinc passivation with intervening water wash and scrub.

Precoating. A solvent-based primer is applied to both sides of the strip by means of a reverse roll coater.

First oven. The sheet is now suspended (under tension) in a large oven (temperature 260 °C) moving at a maximum speed of 30 m/min. Electronic signalling ensures a nearly constant catenary for the strip so that the vaporisation of solvents from the coatings can take place. These solvents are incinerated to prevent atmospheric pollution. The heat generated from the combustion of these solvents is returned via a heat exchanger to preheat the fresh air circulating in the ovens.

Base coat or top coat application. The principal coating is now applied using rubber rollers if both sides of the sheet are to be painted. A second oven then cures this coat. Electronic signalling of the approach of the stitched joint enables the operative to raise the paint applicator rolls to avoid damage to the roller surface by the joint.

The speed of the sheet through the second oven controls the overall speed of the line. It is dictated by tensioning rollers which control the catenary in the

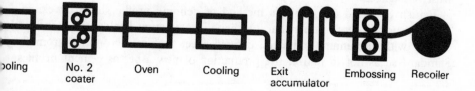

oling   No. 2   Oven   Cooling   Exit   Embossing   Recoiler
           coater   accumulator

second oven to ensure the sheet is suspended correctly and is evenly heated on both sides of the sheet.

An accumulator allows a 1½ min delay at the end of the line and a steering mechanism is provided to ensure the sheet is straight in the line. A back tension device allows re-coiling of the sheet and at this stage prepainted sheets can be fed into the line for embossing if required. Sheets are re-coiled prior to being fed into the rolling mill.

Roll form line

The rolling mill consists of a series of adjustable rollers through which the flat sheets are progressively formed into profiled forms. In some cases it is possible to provide lateral profiling by means of a special roller (see Fig. 4.8). Sheets can be cut to length before or after profiling. Typical manufacturing deviation on the width of the sheet is +2 mm.

In forming the painted steel or aluminium strip some faults can occur, such as micro-cracking, fluting, bows or twists. Fluting is a pattern of kinks that occur at the ends of the sheets during rolling. Pre-cut sheets of high-tensile steel are vulnerable to this problem. It can also be caused by excessive amounts of nitrogen in rolled strip, which may need stretch levelling prior to rolling. Bows and twists can also occur with poor rolling.

To avoid micro-cracking MacGregor (1981) recommends that the minimum bend radius should be four times the sheet thickness for aluminium and eight times for galvanised steel.

Relevant standards

Asbestos cement sheeting

Profiled asbestos sheets are supplied in accordance with BS 690 Part 3: 1973 *Corrugated sheets*. Internal linings are supplied in accordance with BS 690 Part 5: 1975 *Lining sheets and panels*. Accessories and fittings are specified in BS 690 Part 6: 1976 *Fittings for use with corrugated sheets*. These Standards all include items on composition, classification, general appearance and finish, characteristics, marking and manufacturers' certification. Reference is also made to BS 4624: 1970 *Methods of test for asbestos cement building products*. This shows apparatus for testing thickness, bending, strength, impermeability, density and frost resistance.

British Standard 690 Part 3's method of defining profile shape by classification of profile depth rather than by shape is interesting. Unlike the Standards dealing with aluminium and steel, defined sheet profiles are omitted from the Standard so as not to inhibit the production of new asbestos cement profiles.

Fig. 4.8 Lateral profiling can be produced by means of a special roller (courtesy of Plannja AB).

The geometric classification also includes tolerances on dimensions. The Standard also refers to CP 143 Part 14 *Corrugated asbestos cement*, now published in a metric edition as BS 5247 Part 14: 1975. It is this Standard which lays down good practice for the use of corrugated asbestos cement in buildings and includes sections on materials and components, design considerations, application, inspection and maintenance. Fixings should be in accordance with BS 1494 Part 1: 1964 *Fixings for sheet, roof and wall covering*.

Steel sheeting

Profiled steel sheets are available in sinusoidal, symmetrical and asymmetrical trapezoidal profiles. Sinusoidal sheets, where the crests and troughs are symmetrical and have the shape of a sine curve are to BS 3083: 1980 *Hot dipped galvanised corrugated steel sheets for general purposes* (Tables I and II), and the application of these sheets is covered in CP 143 Part 10: 1973. However, the majority of architects in the UK specifying precoated steel sheeting are selecting trapezoidal profiles from the manufacturers' catalogues. There is not yet (1980) a comparable British Standard or Code of Practice for profiles other than sinusoidal, and in the absence of a specific standard for trapezoidal cladding profiles the specifier must refer to the more general CP 5427 *Code of practice for performance and loading criteria for profiled sheeting in building*.

British Standard 3083: 1959 for hot-dipped galvanised sheets defines the type of zinc coating and tolerances on the size of the sheets. Profiles are made from galvanised steel sheet to BS 2989: 1975 with or without organic coating, or to BS 1449 Part 1: 1972 when they are not pregalvanised. The usual quality is Z1 and it is recommended that this has a guaranteed yield stress of 220 N/mm², although some manufacturers would claim that they exceed this.

British Standard 2989: 1975 specifies steel grades, coating tests and tolerances on dimension. The application of sinusoidal hot-dipped galvanised sheets is given in CP 143 Part 10: 1973 which deals with materials, design considerations, application, inspection and maintenance. Some information on handling, working, storage and installation is also given in BS 5427: 1976. Manufacturers' own catalogues would offer the specifier clearer instructions on these matters. Some associations such as the National Federation of Roofing Contractors do offer their own design guidance for the application of profiled sheet metal roofing and cladding.

Standard flashings are supplied by cladding contractors and should be of zinc to BS 849: 1939 and not less than 0.8 mm, or lead to BS 1178: 1969 not less than BS code number 4 (20 kg/m), or steel to BS 2989: 1975. Fixings should be to BS 1494 Part 1: 1964.

Aluminium sheeting

British Standard 4868: 1972 *Profiled aluminium sheet for building* only relates to those sheets where the aluminium alloy has been manufactured in accordance with the two standards governing the wrought aluminium and aluminium alloys BS 1470: 1972 and BS 4300 Part 6: 1969. British Standard 1470 discusses general requirements and methods of test for NS3-H8 and BS 4300 deals with NS31-H6 which has a slightly higher tensile strength.

Although these alloys represent those in most common use for building purposes in the UK, where the aluminium is rolled from imported ingot, there are other types of alloys produced by other methods of production, such as continuous cast coil, which are not covered by the Standard. As a consequence, manufacturers producing aluminium profiled sheets from these other alloys (e.g. Granges Aluminium) can only claim that their products are 'manufactured to the internationally agreed equivalent to BS alloy NS3 of various hardnesses' even though, at least according to the manufacturers' catalogues, the tensile strength of these alloys exceeds those covered by the British Standard.

Profiles, dimensions and cover widths are described in BS 4868: 1972 which specifies requirements for materials, a limited range of profiles, dimensions and finish. Unfortunately, this only refers to a very limited range of profiles (mainly sinusoidal). Trapezoidal profiles are generally preferred by architects as they are generally crisper and can produce sharp shadow lines which are useful for breaking up large surfaces. One of the weaknesses of the present Standard is that because it only includes a small range of such profiles it therefore excludes most aluminium sheets which are produced to profile classes not included in the Standard.

Similarly, the Code of Practice (CP 143 Part 15: 1973) giving recommendations for the installation of aluminium, relates in its title to both sheet roof and wall coverings, but in fact mainly refers to its application on roofs and gutters. It also only relates to one alloy NS3 and therefore is not appropriate to all situations. Brief mention is made to the storage and protection of aluminium sheets. But cross-strappings during unloading and timber cross-battens for stacking are not mentioned, nor are there any limits given for the height of the stack. Manufacturers' own guidance would offer the specifier clearer instructions on these matters.

Fixings should comply with the requirements of BS 1494 Part 1: 1964 showing various fixings for sheet roof and wall coverings. British Standard 4174: 1972 gives the same range of requirements for self-tapping screws and metallic drive screws.

Durability

Perhaps the most serious weakness of the existing standards is that they appear to offer no real assurance to the specifier over the durability and life to first maintenance of these organic coatings.

Some information on durability of surface finish and details of life to first maintenance for factory and site-applied finishes on aluminium is contained in Appendix E of BS 5427: 1976, which is a general Code of Practice for performance and loading criteria for profiled weathering sheeting in a range of materials

Table 4.2   Durability of organic finishes on steel and aluminium from BS 5427 : 1976
Appendix E

(a) General characteristics: factory – and site-applied organic finishes on aluminium and primed hot-dip zinc-coated mild steel

Surface finish	Characteristics				
	Scratch resistance	Stain resistance	Colour fastness	Weathering	Chalking resistance
1. Solution vinyl *Min. 20 μm vinyl chloride acetate copolymer*	G	M	P	P	P
2. Alkyds *Min. 20 μm alkyd and oil-free polyester*	G	G	G	G	M
3. Acrylics *Min. 20 μm thermosetting and thermoplastic acrylic copolymers*	G	G	G	M	M
4. PVC organosol *Min. 20 μm PVC homopolymers*	G	M	P	P	P
5. Silicone enamels *Min. 20 μm siliconised versions of acrylics, alkyds and oil-free polyesters*	G	G	G	M	G
6. Fluoropolymers (liquid applied) *Min. 20 μm PVF and PVF₂*	G	E	E	E	E
7. Fluoropolymers (film-applied) *Min. 20 μm PVF and PVF₂*	G	E	E	E	E
8. Vinasol *Min. 75 μm film organic coating PVC homopolymer*	G	M	M	G	M
9. Plastisol *Min. 175 μm film organic coating PVC homopolymer liquid-applied*	G	G	G	G	G
10. PVC film *Min. 175 μm film organic coating PVC homopolymer-bonded laminates*	G	G	G	G	G
11. Acrylic film *Min. 50 μm film high molecular weight acrylic*	M	G	E	E	E
12. Polyester on asbestos/ metal composite *Min. 100 μm film oil-free polyester*	G	G	G	G	E

Note: E excellent, G good, M moderate, P poor.

Recommendations for life requirements are based on a relatively high aesthetic standard, especially chalking resistance and colour retention, except in the inaccessible environment.
★ May be used with caution.

116

(b) Life to first maintenance (in UK): factory – and site-applied finishes on pretreated aluminium

Surface finish	Type of environment					
	External			Internal		
	Coastal	Industrial and urban	Suburban and rural	Wet and possibly polluted	Dry and unpolluted	Inaccessible enclosed in dry cavity
1. Solution vinyl *Min. 20 μm vinyl chloride acetate copolymer*	S	S	L	M	VL	VL
2. Alkyds *Min. 20 μm alkyds and oil-free polyester*	L	L	L	M	VL	VL
3. Acrylics *Min. 20 μm thermosetting and thermoplastic acrylic copolymers*	L	L	L	M	VL	VL
4. PVC organosol *Min. 20 μm PVC homopolymers*	S★	S	L	M	VL	VL
5. Silicone enamels *Min. 20 μm siliconised versions of acrylics, alkyds and oil-free polyesters*	L	L	L	L	VL	VL
6. Fluoropolymers *Min. 20 μm (liquid-applied) PVF and PVF$_2$*	L	L	L	L★	VL	VL
7. Fluoropolymers *Min. 20 μm (film-applied) PVF and PVF$_2$*	L	L	L	L★	VL	VL
8. Vinasol	—	—	—	—	—	—
9. Plastisol *Min. 175 μm film PVC homopolymer liquid-applied*	M★	L	L	L★	VL	VL
10. PVC film *Min. 175 μm film PBC homopolymer-bonded laminates*	M★	L	L	L★	VL	VL
11. Acrylic film *Min. 50 μm film high molecular weight acrylic*	L	L	L	L★	VL	VL
12. Polyester on asbestos/metal composite *Min. 100 μm film oil-free polyester*	—	—	—	—	—	—

Notes Life to first maintenance:
S short 2– 5 years
M medium 5–10 years
L long 10–20 years

VL very long 20–50 years
— no information or not applicable

117

used in building (see Table 4.2). There is some disagreement within the industry on the basis for the data given in these tables, and the Code states that the data should only be regarded as a guide and that the manufacturer should be consulted for each specific application and environment. It is interesting to note that in the PSA Method of Building (1979), technical guidance on sheet cladding, which was issued a year later than BS 5427 in consultation with the aluminium industry, the same data are given but with a variety of amendments. Out of 50 items included in BS 5427 for durability of organic finishes there are 2 amendments, and out of 60 items for life to first maintenance for organic finishes there are 25 amendments to the tables.

Allowable tolerance in matching colours also needs clarification. British Standard 4904: 1978 *External cladding colours for building purposes* relates colours in terms of hue, greyness and weight, but no mention is made in this document of the performance of different colours or, indeed, of their relative colour fastness. Matching is mentioned under item 5 of this document, but no tolerances on matching are given for guidance by the specifier on what are the limits of acceptability from one batch of coloured sheet to another. Even a cross-reference to BS 3900 Part D1: 1970 *Visual comparison of the colour of paints* would be useful in this respect.

Some manufactures state permissible deviations in colour change of $\triangle E$ to be 1 or less where

$$\triangle E = \sqrt{\triangle L^2 + \triangle a^2 + \triangle b^2}$$

This equation expresses mathematically the deviations in colour caused by differences in L (brightness), a (red/green) and b (yellow/blue), the parameters which are used to define colour. The sum of the deviations E takes account of the statistical probability that they will not be at their worst at any one time. Commercially it may be difficult to control all these factors to the same extent and, for example, the b factor could be a consistent variable and still allow E to be within the rule.

Finishes for metal sheeting

Sheet steel

Profiled steel sheet is available with a variety of finishes. The principal types for cladding are:

Hot-dipped galvanising
This is a zinc finish, which may be spangled or matt.

Hot-dipped zinc/aluminised steel
This is a coating (aluminium finish) consisting of an alloy of approx. 55 per cent aluminium/45 per cent zinc, normally sold as Galvalume, Zincalume or Aluzinc.

It is slightly more expensive than galvanising, but offers better corrosion resistance.

Polyvinyl chloride on hot-dipped galvanising
PVC organosol is no longer in widespread use and the most common finish is PVC Plastisol which can be liquid applied or used as a bonded laminate. The surface will invariably be textured or embossed. This can be considered as a 'thick' coating material with typical nominal thickness of 200 µm.

Acrylic or silicone enamels on hot dipped galvanising
Typically 20 µm with a smooth texture, this offers a different colour range from PVC. Siliconised versions of acrylics are also available and modified silicone and acrylic finishes are now being used, particularly in the USA as thin 'premium' coatings.

Fluoropolymers on hot dipped galvanising
Polyvinylidene fluorides PVF and PVF_2 are also in widespread use as 'thinner' coatings (typically 20 µm) which offer good resistance to weathering. They are usually a mixture of PVF_2 and acrylic and their performance will depend upon the particular formulation applied.

Acrylic modified polyester resin over bitumen/asbestos bonded to steel
This is a very thick coating (overall thickness 500 µm) which is heavily textured and offered in a range of colours, e.g. Galbestos (not now available).

Acrylic modified polyester on an epoxy base
This is a 'thick' coating offering good weathering characteristics (e.g. H. H. Robertson's 'Versacor').

The thicker PVC coatings (Plastisol) offer a better resistance to wear and abrasion than the thinner fluoropolymers (PVF_2) and silicone enamels: however, the PVC colours are not so stable and tend to fade in ultraviolet light. A general rule might be to use PVC in areas where surface wear might be expected, i.e. roofs, and to use the fluoropolymers where colour integrity is important for reasons of appearance, i.e. walls.

In order to prevent discoloration and deterioration of the organic paint finish, particularly with PVC coatings, it is important that the temperature in use should not exceed the safe temperature ranges of the finishes used. Typical safe temperature ranges for different organic coatings are:

PVC (inc. Plastisol)   50 °C to +79 °C
Acrylics   50 °C to 100 °C
Fluoropolymers (inc. PVF_2)   50 °C to 120 °C
Acrylic polyester   50 °C to 70 °C

Dark-coloured sheets, such as chocolate brown, cause the most problems in heat build-up, particularly those with an insulation layer immediately behind the

Fig. 4.9 Delamination of outer paint finish due to heat build-up.

sheet. Generally, black and dark colours can be expected to reach temperatures of 80 °C during summer conditions, medium colours 65 °C and white or bright aluminium 50 °C.

At the Second International Conference on the durability of building materials and components at Washington, USA, 1981, D. A. Thomas explained that it was generally recognised that organic coatings are permeable to water and oxygen, and also to ions, so even a defect-free coating could not be expected to give permanent protection in sufficiently active environments (National Bureau of Standards, 1981). Thus the quality of the primer coating is critical to the durability of the paint finish. At the same conference, C. Christ showed results of test carried out on two paint systems, an acrylic and a modified fluoropolymer with various types of zinc and aluminium substrates. The aluminium-coated substrate was rated better than all other painted substrates at three of four exposure sites. The thickness and weight of the primer is also critical. British Standard 3083: 1959 defines the types of zinc coatings and tolerances on the sizes of sheets for hot-dipped galvanised corrugated sheets. Test methods are also given for determining the weight of zinc. Generally sheeting with the heavier zinc or aluminium coatings beneath the paint films will suffer from less overall deterioration than those with lighter metallic coating weights.

Aluminium

The aluminium industry has always insisted that their material does not need painting as it has its own built-in protective surface coating of aluminium oxide which forms immediately on exposure to the atmosphere. However, in order to compete with the colours of paint finishes available for steel cladding, manufacturers have produced a number of organic coated colour finishes for aluminium sheets. Colour anodising is limited in that it only really offers black, grey, gold or bronze finishes.

Thus profiled aluminium sheet is available with mill finish, anodised, or with an organic coating. Mill finish is a natural oxidised surface which darkens with age. Anodised finishes are generally about 25 μm thick according to BS 3987: 1964 and BS 1615: 1972. There are five different methods of colour anodising:

1. Organic dyes which do not penetrate deeply into the anodic film and are therefore vulnerable to abrasion. Many of these are as light fast as inorganic pigments: some start to fade within two years.
2. Inorganic pigments which are used for gold and bronze finishes.
3. Electrolytic colour which is deposited deeper than organic dyes to produce black, bronze and grey finishes that resist ultraviolet radiation and abrasion.
4. Integral or hard colour, where organic acids produce results similar to the electrolytic process.
5. Special alloys which produce a grey or gold finish during anodising.

Most profiled aluminium sheets are now supplied with organic coatings similar to that previously described for steel. One major difference is that British Aluminium uses an alkyd-amino supplied by ICI, stoved-on in the factory – *after forming* – as 'Baco Colourbond'. Other aluminium sheeting manufacturers favour the fluoropolymers. Alcan use PVF_2 acrylic paint known as Alcan 'Duralcote', Granges Essem also use PVF in their 'Metallack' finish.

The important thing to realise is that the stoved-on alkyd finish has to be done *after forming*, whereas the PVF_2 and acrylics can be applied *before forming*. The implication of this is that whereas with PVF_2 and acrylics, sheets of organic coated materials can be supplied to the fabricator for forming into special flashings and trim, with alkyd finish the flashings have to be fabricated and then sent back to the manufacturer (Baco) for colour coating.

The safe temperature range for aluminium is $-80\,°C$ to $+100\,°C$ above which gradual loss of strength occurs. Above these temperature ranges the colour coating will also discolour and deteriorate. Some colours reflect or absorb heat more than others and dark colours are more likely to reach much higher surface temperatures than light colours. It is important to obtain assurances from the manufacturer on the relative durability, colour fastness and temperature limitations of the various colours available. Further advice on the painting of aluminium is given in BRE Digest No. 71, *Painting: Non-ferrous metals and coatings*.

For both aluminium and steel profiled sheeting, colour matching between batches of sheets and flashings is often a problem. Samples of the limits of colour change can be approved before ordering, but some mismatch of colours on a large job is inevitable. The selection of neutral colours for sheeting or contrasting colours for flashings is a way of overcoming this difficulty.

Performance criteria

The acoustic, thermal, strength, and behaviour in fire criteria are compared for asbestos cement, steel and aluminium in Tables 4.3 and 4.4.

Generally the mean value for airborne sound reduction through profiled sheeting is not better than 28 dB unless additional insulation is provided with

Table 4.3 Performance of cladding materials

Asbestos cement	Steel	Aluminium
Acoustic		
A mean value for airborne sound reduction through a 6 mm sheet is 26 dB.	A mean value for airborne sound reduction through 1.6 mm mild steel sheet is 28 dB. Additional insulation can be provided by a back-up construction. An insulated cladding, such as 9 mm plasterboard, 25 mm mineral wool and profiled steel sheet has a mean sound reduction index of 36 dB. The same construction without mineral wool has 30.9 dB reduction. A steel lining tray with 12.5 mm urethane in place of plasterboard and mineral wool offers 31.5 dB; 75 mm mineral wool insulation and foam sealing strips offer 32.9 dB.	A mean value for airborne sound reduction through 1.6 mm aluminium sheet is 18 dB.
Thermal		
The conductivity (k) for asbestos cement sheet is 0.400 W/m °C. Typical U-values for common wall constructions are given in Table 4.4	The conductivity (k) for carbon steel is 50 W/m °C. Typical U-values for steel sheeting given in Table 4.4	The conductivity (k) for a typical aluminium alloy is 160 W/m °C. To calculate thermal transmittance (U) see BRE Digest 108 *Standard U-values*. Aluminium foil increases insulation only if it faces a cavity.

Table 4.3 (*cont'd.*)

Asbestos cement	Steel	Aluminium

Strength

Sheets are classified by their minimum loadbearing capacity, which depends on whether their profile is symmetrical or asymmetrical, and also by their bending strength. Whatever the loadbearing capacity, sheets should have a minimum bending strength of 15.7 MN/m^2 (symmetrical) or 19.6 MN/m^2 (asymmetrical) when tested to BS 4624. This does not apply to curved or cranked sheets. Further data on sampling and testing are given in BS 690 Part 3 and BS 5427.

Figures published in manufacturers' trade literature are not necessarily comparable. Plannja, for example, use high tensile steel for their profiles which increases the permissible span across supports, BSC in describing the properties of their profile make reference to BS 2989: 1975. Manufacturers should be asked to explain the basis of their calculations. BS 5427 permits deflections of span/90.

The tensile strength of the two main aluminium alloys used in the UK is: BS 1470 – Ns 3 – 1 175 N/mm^2; BS 4300/6 – NS31 – H6, 185 N/mm^2 (BS 4868). Thin aluminium may damage easily on-site, particularly from ladders or equipment.

Behaviour in fire

Asbestos cement cladding has no fire resistance as defined in BS 476: Part 8. Where fire resistance is required, asbestos cement can be used with a suitable fire-resisting lining, such as asbestos insulation board to BS 3536, plasterboard or mineral fibre insulating board, to which the performance can be found in Schedule 8 of the Building Regulations 1976.

Profiled steel cladding has no fire resistance as defined in BS 476: Part 8. Where fire resistance is required, steel sheet can be used with a suitable fire-resisting lining. Profiled steel sheet is classified as 'not easily ignitable' (p) to BS 476 Part 5 and 'non-combustible' to BS 476 Part 4. Profiled steel sheet without a finish can be graded as Class 0 surface spread of flame classification. For classification of sheets with proprietary coatings, the manufacturer should be consulted and if required a test certificate obtained.

Profiled aluminium sheet cladding has no fire resistance as defined in BS 476 Part 8. It is classified as 'not easily ignitable' (p) to BS 476 Part 5 and 'not combustible' to BS 476 Part 4. Aluminium sheeting with mill finish can be graded as Class O spread of flame. For classification of sheets with a proprietary coating it would be necessary to obtain a test certificate from the manufacturer concerned. Obviously it can be used as a total fire-resistant construction with a suitable back-up material.

Table 4.4 Thermal performance. – typical U values

Material	Construction	U-value W/m^2 °C
Asbestos	1. Single asbestos cement sheet	5.3
	2. As (1), but with 20 mm cavity and aluminium foil-backed plasterboard lining	1.8
	3. Double-skin asbestos cement with 50 mm glass fibre insulation in between	1.0
	No allowance has been made for the effect of corrugations on heat loss.	
Steel	1. Plastic-covered steel sheet	5.7
	2. As (1), but with cavity and aluminium foil-backed plasterboard lining	1.9
Aluminium	1. Bright surface inside and outside	2.6
	2. Dull surface outside bright surface inside	2.8
	3. As (1), but with cavity and aluminium foil-backed plasterboard lining	1.8
	4. As (2), but with cavity and aluminium foil-backed plasterboard lining.	1.9

a back-up construction of mineral wool, in which case it is possible to achieve 36 dB. With such a construction U values of 1.8 W/m^2 °C are normally possible.

In considering strength, steel and aluminium profiled sheeting can be designed to withstand a deflection of span/90. Since the performance of cladding is often determined by the deflection criteria, the limit chosen is important. Most manufacturers now consider that a limit of span/90 does not represent good roofing practice and is likely to lead to troubles from leaks developing at laps. Thus moves are being made to introduce more stringent controls for roof sheeting. Test rigs for the measurement of the strength of metal profiled sheeting as included in BS 5427 measurement of bending strength of corrugated asbestos sheeting as included in BS 4624 are shown in Fig. 4.1.

A comprehensive description of performance criteria for wall and roof cladding is given in the CEGB (1970) guide which includes sections on loading and strength, fire rating, thermal insulation and acoustic properties.

Resistance to hard body impact is another important characteristic of metal cladding systems and manufacturers should be asked for results of impact tests (see Fig. 4.11).

Installation

Most manufacturers include guidance in their trade literature on the method of handling and storage of their material on-site. All the profiled metal manufacturers depend upon nominated subcontractors for the detailed design and erection of their cladding. The quality of workmanship on-site, particularly at the edge of sheets and the method of fixing, are important factors in the proper

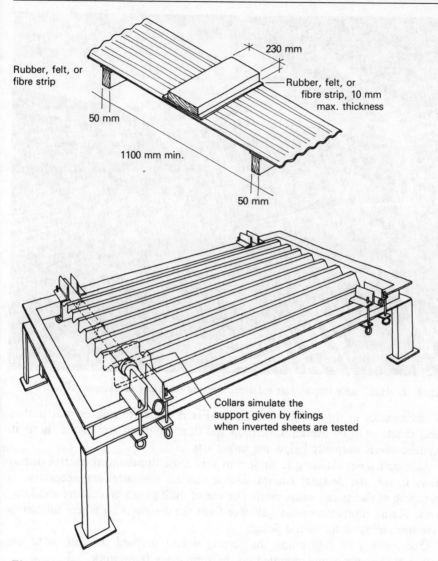

Fig. 4.10 Test rigs for measurement of the strength of metal profiled and corrugated asbestos sheeting (courtesy of British Standards Institution: (a) based on Fig. 6 of BS 4624: 1981; and (b) is based on Fig. 2 of BS 5427: 1976, with permission).

assembly of profiled sheeting. Edges of sheets crumpled in handling can look unsightly. The present vogue of using profiled metal horizontally (see Fig. 4.12) imposes an even greater requirement for care in the assembly and fixing of flashings and trims.

One of the advantages of profiled sheet metal cladding is that, with care, the fixing subcontractors can adjust the setting out of their sheets to take account

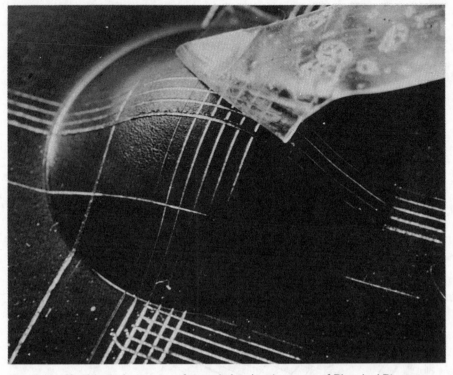

Fig. 4.11 Hard body impact test for steel sheeting (courtesy of Plannja AB).

of inaccuracies in the structural framing. Fixers prefer to pull on rather than bend sheets to fit an overall dimension and thus the mean size of the sheets in manufacture is normally below the target size.

Although sheet cladding is subject to very close dimensional control during manufacture, the designer cannot assume that no tolerances are necessary, as spreading of sheets can cause cutting or use of infill pieces on corners and junctions. Fixing contractors need guidance from the designers on where tolerances have been allowed for in the design.

One method of controlling the setting out of profiled sheeting is to use setting-out or spacer jigs mounted on the supporting framework.

The minimum height of stacking profiled sheets on-site can be important in reducing the effect of spreading of the overall width of those sheets at the bottom of the stack. Even the way in which the units are lifted on and off the lorry can affect the dimension if they are not crated correctly.

Effect of temperature change on fixings

The external surface of aluminium sheeting will have to withstand a maximum daily temperature range of 50 °C if mill finish or light coloured, and up to 70 °C

Fig. 4.12 Profiled sheeting used horizontally (courtesy Plannja Dobel Ltd).

if dark coloured. As the coefficient of linear expansion of aluminium is 23 × 10^{-6} °C, these temperature ranges mean that an 8 m long sheet will expand about 10 mm and 13 mm for light and dark-coloured sheets respectively. It is necessary to accommodate this movement on dark-coloured sheets by oversize holes or non-rigid fixings, but no special requirements are necessary for light-coloured or mill finish sheets. Over 8 m in length, non-rigid fixings should always be used. There is no need to provide expansion joints across the width of the sheet as the profile will accommodate movement. For steel sheets, the coefficient of linear expansion of steel is 12 × 10^{-6} °C means that an 8 m long sheet will expand 5–7 mm. The inherent flexibility of the material can accommodate this, but over 8 m non-rigid fixings should be used.

The safe temperature range for asbestos cement sheets is −25 °C to 200 °C, but note that an applied finish may not accommodate this range. The manufacturer should guarantee performance over the range specified for the project. The external surface of the sheeting must withstand a maximum daily temperature range of 40 °C. As the coefficient of linear expansion of asbestos cement is 8 × 10^{-6} °C, this 40 °C range means that a 3 m long sheet will expand about 1 mm. Non-rigid fixings must therefore be used for any length of sheet. Thermal movement across the sheet requires an expansion joint for any continuous run between 45 and 75 m, with a further joint every 30 m thereafter.

Position of fixings

Primary fixings in asbestos cement sheets should be made through the crown of the corrugations except where sheets are fixed to cold rolled steel rails, as they tend to slide downwards through leverage on the fixings. In this case, some manufacturers recommend that sheets should be fixed through the valley (see Fig. 4.13). This method of fixing is weaker and should be taken into account when calculating wind loading. For example, one manufacturer recommends a reduction of 15 per cent in the figures for suction loading permitted for crown fixings.

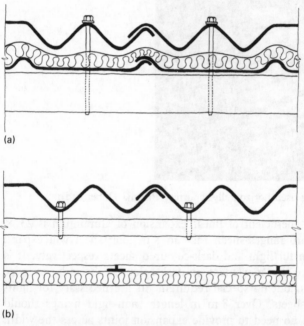

(a)

(b)

Fig. 4.13 Fixing positions using asbestos cement sheets: (a) crown fixings to hot-rolled steel sladding rails; (b) valley fixings to cold-rolled steel cladding rails.

Using metal sinusoidal sheeting, primary fixing should be made through the crown of the corrugations. However, using trapezoidal metal sheeting, fixing in the crown of the profiles can cause spreading of the sheets and damage to the metal and thus it is normally advisable to fix in the troughs (see Fig. 4.14). Maximum fixing centres are 450 mm or every third corrugation, whichever is the less.

Secondary fixings secure one sheet to another so as to exclude wind and rain and provide continuity from sheet to sheet for the dispersion of applied loads. For wall claddings the shear strength of fixings in the centre of the crown is usually adequate, provided that they are no further than 500 mm apart. In some

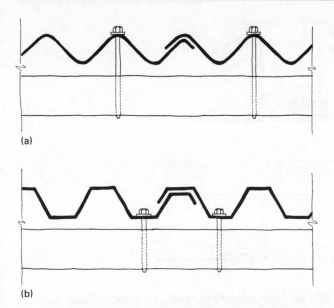

(a)

(b)

Fig. 4.14   Fixing positions using steel or aluminium sheets: (a) crown fixings for sinusoidal sheeting; (b) trough fixings for trapezoidal sheeting.

cases it may be possible to provide secret fixings at the side laps between sheets
(see Fig. 4.15).

Types of fixings

Primary fixings attaching metal cladding to steel rails are commonly self-tapping
screws (see Fig. 4.16).

Primary fixings which attach asbestos cement to vertical cladding to steel rails
should be of the hook bolt, or bolt and clip type, as described in BS 1494: Part
1 (see Fig. 4.17).

Direct fixing of sheets by stud welding or by self-tapping screws to metal
framing should not be used for asbestos cement cladding, as it tends to restrain
sheeting movement unduly and causes it to crack, nor should cartridge fasteners
be used.

Blind light rivets are usually used for secondary fixings in metal claddings.
For steel sheeting, cadmium-plated Monel metal rivets should be used, not
cadmium-plated mild steel. Rivets in aluminium sheeting should be aluminium
alloy (see Fig. 4.18).

Cartridge-assisted fasteners, as shown in Fig. 4.19, are used to secure metal
roof deck units, but are not used where watertightness relies upon careful tightening against a washer seal such as is required when fixing roof and wall cladding
sheets. Welded or screwed stud fixings for impaled sheets should not be used
for metal sheet cladding.

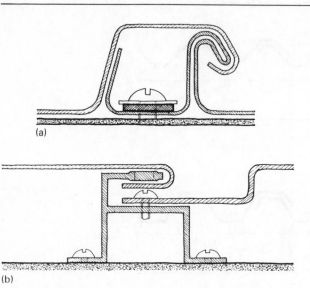

Fig. 4.15 Examples of side lap joints with secret fixings: (a) fixings without accessory section; (b) fixing with accessory section.

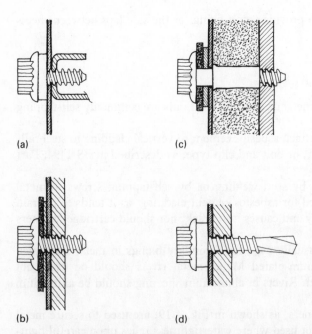

Fig. 4.16 Examples of self-tapping screws: (a) 12 point plastic head type 'Z' cone pointed screw with sealing ring to BS 1494: Part 1 Fig. 17; (b) modified version of (a) with load spreading head; (c) modified version of (b) with spacing collar; (d) self-drilling screw.

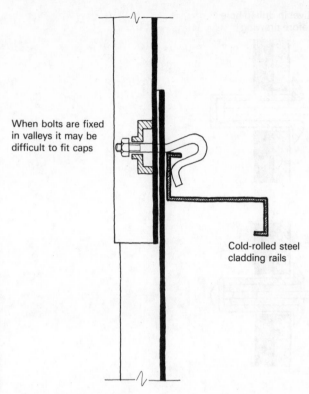

When bolts are fixed
in valleys it may be
difficult to fit caps

Cold-rolled steel
cladding rails

Fig. 4.17 Cranked hook bolts for use with asbestos cement sheets and cold-rolled steel rails.

Secondary fixings are not required with asbestos cement sheeting for fastening side laps and end laps. Their use in vertical cladding is generally for fixing accessory sheets, when this is not possible with primary fixings, and for double cladding. For these purposes the BS type roofing bolt, with washer and cap is suitable.

Fixings should comply with the requirements of BS 1494 Part 1: 1964 showing various fixings for sheet roof and wall coverings. Also useful is the CEGB design guide (1970) which shows (by photographs) the actual size of the fixing devices.

Sheet cladding may fail at the fixings either by pull through or by failure of the fixing itself. Fixing should therefore be specified to include nuts, washers and weather-seal devices, all preferably from the same manufacturer.

Compatibility with other materials

Compatibility with other materials is also an important consideration, particularly when using aluminium.

131

Rivet after drawing
and stern snapped

Rivet in drilled hole
before drawing

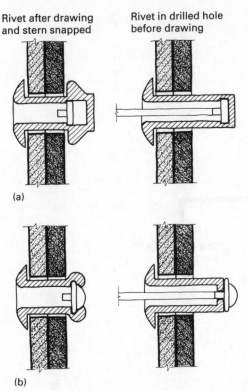

(a)

(b)

Fig. 4.18 Rivets for secondary fixings in metal cladding: (a) pop rivet; (b) sealed-end rivet.

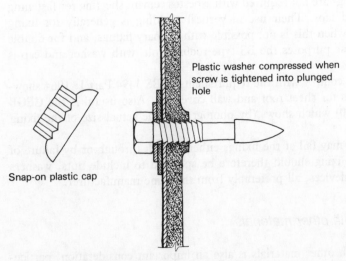

Plastic washer compressed when
screw is tightened into plunged
hole

Snap-on plastic cap

Fig. 4.19 Cartridge fasteners for metal cladding.

Aluminium is particularly susceptible to electrolytic corrosion with dissimilar materials. With an organic coating, it is liable to attack if pierced or cut, and anodised aluminium is as susceptible as the untreated metal. There is no corrosive action between aluminium and zinc or zinc coatings and galvanising.

Aluminium sheeting, whether organically coated or not, suffers attack from many building materials. Direct contact should be avoided by good detailing and efficient drainage to prevent water run-off. In unavoidable, the following protective measures can be taken:

Copper alloys	No protective measures possible; avoid direct contact and water run-off from copper on to aluminium, unless organically coated.
Iron and steel	*Direct contact.* Unless organically coated, use non-aggressive protective paint, e.g. zinc chromate. Avoid copper-bearing paints. In industrial and marine atmospheres, non-rotting chromate insulating tape. *Water run-off.* Paint iron, galvanise and paint steel (non-copper-bearing, non-aggressive paint).
Lead	Unless organically coated, avoid contact and run-off.
Timber	Compatible non-copper-based preservative (see CP 143) bituminous paint or felt or building paper.
Boards	Moisture barrier, such as building paper or polythene.
Concrete, plaster asbestos cement	Bituminous paint and felt insert between contact surfaces.

Hot-dip zinc-coated steel suffers moderate attack from copper alloys, iron, steel, some timbers, cement, concrete, plaster, asbestos cement, copper-bearing paints and stainless steel, particularly if water run-off from material on to this cladding occurs. Direct contact should be avoided by good detailing, and efficient drainage will prevent run-off.

Organic coatings on hot-dip zinc-coated steel are unaffected by all common building materials, unless they are cut or pierced, when they behave similarly to hot-dip zinc-coated sheet.

Joints between sheets

Side laps of one corrugation will generally prevent driving rain passing through the outer cladding, but when exposure is 'severe' as defined in BRE Digest 127 (e.g. in areas with a driving rain index of seven or more) an increased lap may be needed (see Fig. 4.20).

Side laps may sometimes need to be increased locally to avoid cutting sheets at corners and openings. Such laps are easy to increase with regular profiles, but

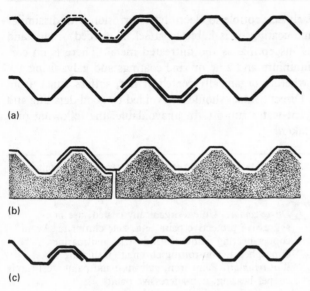

(a)

(b)

(c)

Fig. 4.20 Side laps between sheets: (a) maximum flexibility in side laps is provided by sheets with uniform troughs and half-corrugations; (b) standard sheets with factory-bonded backings do not permit variations in side lap; (c) sheets in which corrugations are not uniform do not allow variations in side lap.

are difficult with irregular profiles and sheets with bonded insulation.

End lap joints on walls will normally be 100 mm and on roofs, 150 mm, but when exposure is severe the end lap should be increased to 200 mm.

As horizontal laps will always show, particularly with dirt deposition – see for example the horizontal laps at Wallingford (see Fig. 4.1) – this must either be accepted, or preferably, full height sheets should be used. The effect of corrugations is lost at 100 to 150 m although it still affects texture. Weathering will affect the overall design and the detail, and local dirt deposits and streaking can be avoided by ensuring uniform washing from water run-off. Sills specifically require special detailing to avoid unsightly staining below. Weathering on the underside of profiles, where sheets are used horizontally, can be reduced by using smaller profiles.

Sealing of lap joints with mastic is not generally used in vertical sheeting for weather protection. However, sealed side laps are required for pitched roof cladding below 15° pitch (see Falconer, 1981). Swedish building practice HusAMA also recommends weather seals for profiled sheet roofing for pitches below 14° and requires side laps to be joined with screws with washers to protect from leakage, or rivets maximum centre to centre 500 mm. Corner details are an important design consideration. Figure 4.21 shows various ways of turning a corner using flashings. Over-sheet corner flashings usually need to be wide in relation to the profile of the main cladding and tend to conflict with it in scale. Appearance and weathering are improved by inverting the edges of the angle,

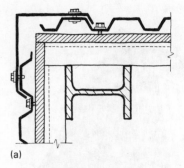

(a)

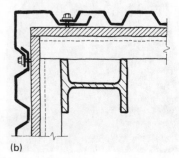

(b)

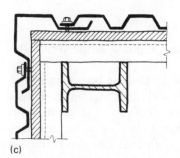

(c)

Fig. 4.21 Various methods of corner detailing using flashings: (a) over-sheet corner flashing; (b) over- and under-sheet corner flashing; (c) under-sheet corner flashing.

but this allows little flexibility in positioning the sheets with the profile shown. Curved-over-sheet corner flashings can also be used.

Using over- and under-sheet corner flashings, these can be shaped to match the profile of the main cladding. The upturned lip of the main cladding is also covered, offering a better water check.

With under-sheet flashings, in order to avoid the exposure of an upturned lip, one of the cladding sheets has been reversed. The length of the under leg of the flashing offers some tolerance in the assembly. In some cases the sheets

135

Fig. 4.22 Corner detail with exposed steel frame (courtesy of Plannja Dobel Ltd).

are butted against the steel frame and the frame exposed at the corner (see Fig. 4.22).

With horizontal cladding, various corner-joint details have been used including welded corners and special GRP closer ends with matching finish, as used at IBM Greenford (architects: Foster Associates). Tolerances in manufacture and assembly are even more critical with horizontal cladding as any misalignment of the profiles can cause apparent waving. Slip trays can also be used at the joints between horizontal cladding; however, it is sometimes difficult to match the profiles exactly and the thickness of the slip tray tends to make the edge of the sheet more obvious in appearance.

Profiled sheeting is best used in well-proportioned large areas, to enclose the main structure with the minimum of joints with other materials. Translucent sheets are available to match most profiles. If opening lights or transparent areas are required, stretches of patent glazing are better than small isolated windows, because they relate more naturally to the scale of the main cladding and reduce the problem of jointing around window openings.

Butt-end joints between sheeting and windows are normally made with Z-flashings. Figure 4.23 shows the recent introduction of a patent neoprene flashing (Corriseal) around a projecting window opening in profiled metal by Essex Aluminium Co. Ltd.

Fig. 4.23   Corriseal neoprene flashing (courtesy of Essex Aluminium Co. Ltd).

Sheeting rails and liner trays

The optimum use of sheeting rails to support profiled cladding is critical to the economic use of the material and its capacity to withstand wind loading. Constrado (1980) shows typical spans of around 2 m for profiled steel cladding, depending upon its profile. Thus sheeting rails are required at intervals up the height of the wall to support the cladding. These sheeting rails must themselves be designed to span between the main support columns (see Fig. 4.24).

As an alternative to sheeting rails, liner trays can be used which when clipped together (see Fig. 4.25) act as horizontal rails at 500 mm intervals. The interaction of cladding and liner trays provides a composite lattice effect. Mineral fibre insulation can be pushed into the liner trays from the outside before the outer profiled cladding is fixed. The flat surface of the liner tray, which can be

137

Fig. 4.24 Sheeting rails are needed to span between main supports (courtesy J. Boswell).

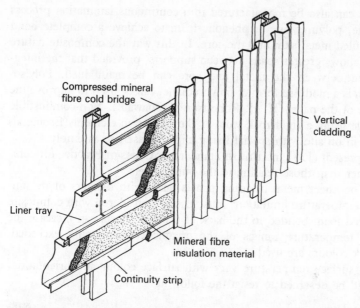

Compressed mineral
fibre cold bridge

Vertical
cladding

Liner tray

Mineral fibre
insulation material

Continuity strip

Fig. 4.25   Liner tray assembly.

prepainted, then acts as a finished inner lining to the construction. Such liner trays are available from European Profiles or Plannja and can either be used horizontally as described above, or vertically, used in conjunction with horizontal profiled cladding.

Composite units

It is always difficult in any design of a cladding system to ensure continuity of the insulation, particularly at the wall to sloping roof junction and gutter detail.

Present legislation on energy conservation has encouraged the development of 'insulated' or 'composite' sheeting, and most manufacturers of steel and aluminium sheetings will also offer a rigid non-loadbearing cladding panel incorporating a thermal insulating material. In its simplest form, this consists of a profiled metal skin to which is bonded a rigid polymeric foam which may have a thin, flexible, smooth lining bonded to the internal face. The spaces formed by the profiles are not normally filled with rigid sheet foam. The adhesives are usually neoprene or urethane. Isocyanurate is a modified form of polyurethane.

The joint between the units is normally achieved by conventional overlapping of the outer profiled sheets. Products of this type are relatively untried and in the light of limited experience to date, the manufacturers' advice on detailing should be sought and a guaranteed performance agreed.

139

Isolated units can also be manufactured in a continuous lamination process using polystyrene, polyurethane or phenolic foam to achieve a complete bond between the profiled metal skin and the core. In this way the composite nature of the assembly allows greater spans between supports, provided that the integrity of the bond between the metal and core can be maintained. Polyisocyanurate, which is a modified form of polyurethane, can be used to improve the fire performance of the panel (H. H. Robertson 'Trimawall'). Non-combustible units are possible using a rigid rock wool as the insulation element (Ecometal) which is placed in on site with special fixing clips to ease site assembly.

There are at present (1981) no British Standard or Codes of Practice for composite units, other than those relating to the outer sheets.

The chapter on sheet metal cladding panels deals with dangers of delamination. Surface temperature limitations must also be considered with composite units, as insulated foam bonded to the back of profiled sheets can increase the danger of safe temperature ranges of the organic coating being exceeded, especially if dark colours are used.

The external surface temperature vary with surface colour and orientation. Claddings should be designed to resist the following:

Black and dark colours	80°C
Medium colours	65°C
White or bright aluminium	50°C

The possible minimum external surface temperature is −20 °C. These temperature limits may affect the surface finish, the insulation and the sheet/insulant bond. Bond and insulant performance should be agreed with the manufacturer.

References

British Standards (1976) *Code of Practice for Performance and Loading Criteria for Profiled Sheeting in Building* BS 5427: 1976. British Standards Institution: London.

Brookes, A. J. (1980) 'Claddings 1-Product selection and specification of profiled asbestos cement, steel and aluminium sheets', *Architects' Journal*, 8.10.1980.

Central Electricity Generating Board (1970) 'Design memorandum – wall and roof cladding', 097/117 issue, 2.4.1970.CEGB: London.

Constrado (1981) *Profiled Steel Cladding and Decking for Commercial and Industrial Buildings*, Constrado doc., SMP/38/80.

Falconer, P. (1981) 'Industrial pitched roofs – the art of construction series', *Architects' Journal*, 14.10.1981.

Lyall, S. (1981) 'Profile of a sound idea', *Building Design*, 27.10.1981, 40–5.

MacGregor, I. (1981) 'Coil coating', *Build* No. 29, Oct. 1981, Building Research Association of New Zealand.

Metal Roof Deck Association (1970) *Code of Design and Technical Requirements for 'Light' Gauge Metal Roof Decks*, Metal Roof Deck Association: Sussex.

National Bureau of Standards (1981) *Proceedings of Second International Conference on the Durability of Building Materials and Components'*, Sept. 14–16th 1981. National Bureau of Standards: Gaithersburg, USA.

Property Services Agency Method of Building (1979) *Technical Guidance – Sheet Cladding – Non-loadbearing Profiled Asbestos Cement, Steel and Aluminium*, MOB doc. TP/E09-200 (2nd edn 1979), PSA London.

Chapter 5

Sheet metal cladding panels

Introduction

Early examples of metal cladding systems, mainly in the USA and France, usually consisted of metal undercill panels mounted into curtain walling assemblies known in the USA as 'stick' systems, or in France as *La grille*. In this way a continuous curtain wall could be used, with the metal, solid (non-glazed) panels masking the floors and columns. Such infill panels were often small in size (typically 1.75 m long × 0.75 m high), and were often pressed into a decorative or embossed profile. During the 1950s such systems were in widespread use in multi-storey buildings, typified by the rigid chequer pattern façades produced by the exposed curtain walling framework.

Aesthetic objections to this form of façade, together with improved legislation on energy conservation and insulation, encouraged architects to consider complete panel assemblies where the solid, insulation and opening elements are fabricated on subframes in the factory and transported to the site and erected as one unit.

In Europe the father of pressed metal panel systems is undoubtedly Jean Prouvé (*Architectural Design*, 1963). Many such panel systems, *Le panneau*, have been developed by Prouvé; interesting projects include his early use of metal composite panels at the Aero Club Roland Garros in 1935, and the façade designed for 'Cours Conception Construction', an industrialised school building system designed in 1963 (see Huber and Steinegger, 1971). Many of Prouvé's ideas are still relevant today and there is now considerable experience of the design, production and use of such panels on the Continent, particularly in France, Italy, Belgium and Germany (see Sebestyen, 1977). In the UK there has not been the same demand and therefore the same experience of production of metal composite units, although some UK manufacturers are now investing in suitable forming and pressing facilities, see Brookes (1980).

UK developments

Early developments of steel panels in this country included the Oxford Regional Hospital Board panel (originally produced by Pressings and Stampings Ltd).

This was early days in the use of polyurethane foams and some difficulties were experienced in the foaming of the insulation of these panels and in ensuring the integrity of the skins and the core material. The panel system was later abandoned in favour of a more conventional horizontal profiled high tensile steel cladding with site-applied insulation. The original panel design did incorporate one interesting feature in its panel to panel jointing. A gasket joint (designed by Jan Sliwa) was based on a jointing principle developed by Jean Prouvé in

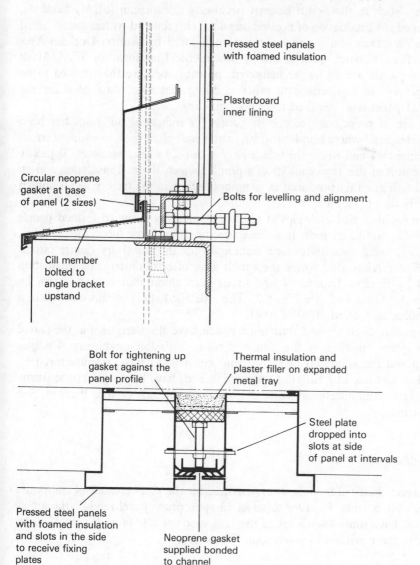

Fig. 5.1 Oxford Regional Health Authority system – panel joint (courtesy Oxford Regional Health Authority).

which a neoprene gasket fixed to a steel channel is compressed against the panel profile by compression bolts at intervals up the height of the panel (see Fig. 5.1).

The economics of using metal composite units depends upon standardisation of unit sizes and it is perhaps not surprising that their use tends to be associated with a system of co-ordinated dimensions. For example, during the 1970s, development in open system tendering by local authority consortia schools programmes, such as the South Eastern Architects Consortium (SEAC Mark 4), encouraged the production of pressed metal panels mounted within a steel 'third member' subframe. Such panels were manufactured by Gordon Durham Aye-cliffe Ltd, as 'Conatus' panels, and by Brockhouse Lightform for SEAC Mark 4. These panels are no longer marketed, probably because they proved to be too expensive in comparison to other cladding materials when used for the variety of panel sizes required for school buildings.

The use of proprietary composite panels for industrial buildings has been more widespread where standard-width panels are bolted back to a simple structural framework and where the façade has no, or only a few, windows. Typically a façade unit of this type consists of a profiled sheet, thermal insulation and an internal lining, either produced as a composite unit in the factory or assembled separately on-site (see Fig. 5.21).

More sophisticated examples of the use of specially designed formed panels in the UK would include those manufactured by Superform Metals ITC, Worcester, using vacuum-forming techniques for the Sainsbury Centre (architects: Foster Associates) where the panels were of box construction (insulation applied by Bradley Laminates) and fixed to an aluminium carrier system by Modern Art Glass Ltd (see Fig. 5.2). For a detailed study of this construction see Brookes and Ward (1981) Part II.

Natural anodised pressed aluminium panels have also been used at the David Murray John building in the Brunel Centre, Swindon (architects: Douglas Stephen and Partners) (Fig. 5.3). Vitreous enamelled panels, manufactured by Escol Ltd and fixed by Crittall Construction Ltd, have been used at the Burne House Telecommunications Centre in London (architects: Charles Pearson, Son and Partners).

Production methods

The correct choice of module size is essential for the economic use of composite metal cladding units. In order to select an appropriate panel module the architect must have some knowledge of the limitations of size of each type of panel related to their method of production. These are:

Fig. 5.2 Sainsbury Centre panels (architects: Foster Associates) (courtesy of J. Platts).

Press braking

Bending of metal sheet in its cold state is a relatively simple process, using a 'brake press', and once a sheet of metal (3 mm or less) has been cut at the corners, it can be formed into a tray and the corners welded. Today brake presses can be computer controlled to produce a wide variety of edge profiles (see Fig. 5.4). The size of the panel produced in this way is limited only by the size of the sheet and the length of the brake press (panels are normally restricted to 4 m × 1.5 m). Finishes, such as anodising, would be applied to these panels after fabrication.

Fig. 5.4   Brake press.

Metal forming

Pressing of sheet metal in one operation is more difficult and the panels formed in this manner in the UK are normally restricted to 2 m × 1 m. Such panels were produced for the parapet units at the Brunel Centre by Dowty Boulton Paul Ltd, and are typical of panels formed by metal-forming techniques. Similarly, the steel panels for the Milton Keynes factory Kiln Farm (architects: Milton Keynes Development Corporation), were also stamped out in one operation (see Fig. 5.30). The 1.8 m × 1.2 m pressed panels for the Sainsbury Centre were produced by TIC Superform by pressing them round a shape using a special alloy of superplast aluminium. Where panels need to be pressed in three dimensions this can be done by 'deep drawing' techniques. For example, panels at the Federal Technical College, Lausanne, Switzerland (architects: Zweifel and Strickler), were drawn into a three-dimensional shape by Schmidlin

Fig. 5.3   Brunel Centre, Swindon (architects: Douglas Stephen/Building Design Partnership).

AG Ltd using a deep-drawn press (see Fig. 5.5). This press has a 6 m × 3 m table capable of taking work pieces up to 5737 mm × 2200 mm and drawing up to 500 mm deep. The presses which are required for deep drawing such panels are not readily available in the UK.

Fig. 5.5   Deep-drawing press (courtesy of Hans Schmidlin AG).

Lamination

Large laminated panels (up to 7 m × 2.5 m) can be pressed together under heat using a *Plattenpress*, where a number of panels can be made up from trays, sheet insulation, edging pieces and backing sheets and stacked together before pressing. Typical of such panels are those produced by Josef Gartner and Co. in Germany, where the outer aluminium sheet is press braked and welded into a dish. Into this is placed a honeycomb core with a further aluminium sheet forming the inner lining. The complete assembly is bonded together with a neoprene or timber edging and placed in a large *Plattenpress* (see Fig. 5.6). In this way

Fig. 5.6 *Plattenpress* (courtesy of Josef Gartner and Co.).

laminated panels can be produced up to 2.5 m × 7.0 m long.

Vacuum presses can also be used to press laminated panels, but because the panels are pressed not more than two at a time the production may be slower; for example, the vacuum press at Crittall Construction Ltd (see Fig. 5.7), can produce sandwich panels with either a mineral fibre, polyurethane or honeycomb core up to 1.6 m × 4.0 m long as standard, and larger sizes may be possible after consultation.

Panels can also be laminated using large 'nip' rollers. Using pressing techniques it is possible, with care, to apply a finish prior to fabrication.

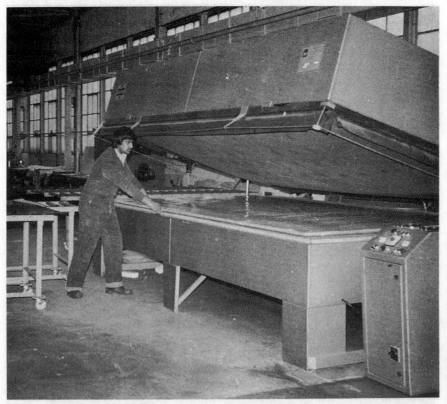

Fig. 5.7 Vacuum press (courtesy of Crittall Construction Ltd).

Curved panels

Curved panels are usually produced in one direction only by cold rolling or pressing. Panels curved in three dimensions can be produced by deep-drawing techniques. Curved laminated panels (see Fig. 5.8) will inevitably cost more than flat panels, as special forms are required to press the panels which will increase their cost of production.

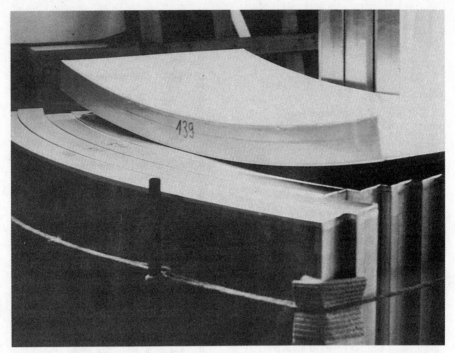

Fig. 5.8   Curved laminated panels.

Thin laminated sheets, such as 'Alucobond' manufactured by Swiss Aluminium Ltd, can be curved to minimum radius of approximately ten times the panel thickness – typical curves 30–80 mm radius.

Curves in deep-drawn panels will be related to the corner radius of the panels and the depth of the drawn tray, and manufacturers' design graphs must be consulted. For a panel of corner radius 150 mm and drawn depth of 115 mm a minimum drawn radius of 10 mm will be required.

Types of metal composite panels

In addition to the simplest form of composite panel in which polymeric foam sheet insulation is bonded to standard profile metal (see Ch. 4), there are essentially four types of exterior metal cladding systems (see Fig. 5.9):-

1. Rolled sheet panels.
2. Box-type panels (including proprietary panels).
3. Laminated panels.
4. Rain screen panels.

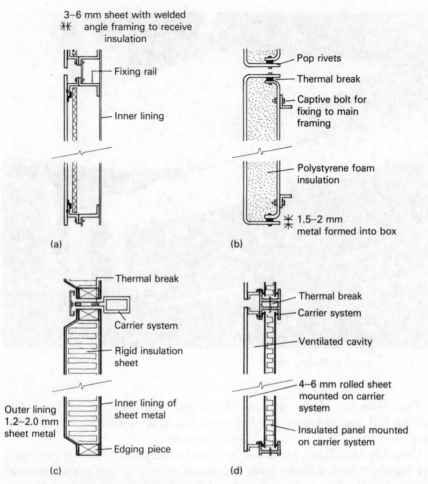

3–6 mm sheet with welded
✳✝ angle framing to receive
insulation

— Fixing rail

— Inner lining

(a)

— Pop rivets

— Thermal break

— Captive bolt for
fixing to main
framing

— Polystyrene foam
insulation

✳ 1.5–2 mm
metal formed into box

(b)

— Thermal break

— Carrier system

— Rigid insulation
sheet

Outer lining
1.2–2.0 mm
sheet metal

— Inner lining of
sheet metal

— Edging piece

(c)

— Thermal break

— Carrier system

— Ventilated cavity

— 4–6 mm rolled sheet
mounted on carrier
system

— Insulated panel mounted
on carrier system

(d)

Fig. 5.9   Types of metal composite panels: (a) rolled sheet panel; (b) box-type panels; (c) laminated panels; (d) rain screen panel.

Rolled sheet panels

This type of panel consists of 3–6 mm sheet metal formed into a metal pan on the outside face, either by cutting and welding the metal into a tray or, more usually, spot welding angles which form the edge to the tray. The stiffness of the panel thus depends upon the thickness of the metal and the number of stiffening angles. (See Fig. 5.10.)

The panel is supported by a fixing rail or some form of secondary framing and the insulation is normally applied loosely on-site, although in some cases it can be glued to the back of the panel in the factory. The inside face is finished either with another metal sheet or a conventional interior finish material such

Fig. 5.10 Stiffening angles to rolled sheet panel.

as gypsum plasterboard. The essential difference between this type of panel and other types described is that the insulation and inner linings do not add to the total stiffness of the panel. One problem in manufacturing such panels is that of avoiding the rippling of the surface or 'oil canning effect' and ensuring the sheet metal is perfectly flat and smooth, which also influences the thickness of the metal used.

In order to allow for thermal expansion of the aluminium rolled sheet, it is now advised that the sheet is not directly connected to the angle framing, but 'floated' on to its supports using Z-section cleats (see Fig. 5.11(a)). These cleats

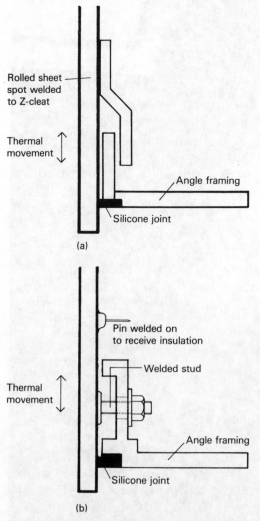

Fig. 5.11 Alternative methods of fixing angle framing to rolled steel panels: (a) Z-section cleat spot welded to sheet; (b) welded stud on outer sheet with slotted holes in angle framing.

are spot welded to the sheet during fabrication, thus holding it within the frame. Following fabrication the edges are sealed with a silicone joint. Pins can also be welded to the back of the sheet on to which the sheets of insulation are mounted.

Many recent (1981) projects in the USA have been constructed using rolled sheet panels. These would include City-Corp building in New York (curtain walling by Flour City), and the Richard J. Hughes Justice complex at Trenton, NJ (architects: The Hillier Group, Princeton), also supplied and erected by Flour City. Such panels were also used at the Federal Reserve Bank building in Boston – see Fig. 5.12 – (architect: Hugh Stubbins), where flanges were welded on to 5 mm plate aluminium and at the Bronx Centre, New York (architect: Richard Meier), where 3 mm aluminium sheet was press braked and the corners formed by cutting and welding into a tray. These were mounted on to a secondary framing on site with insulation and inner linings applied *in situ*. For a detailed description of these projects, see Murphy (1978).

Fig. 5.12   Federal Reserve Bank, Boston (architects: Hugh Stubbins).

The maximum size of rolled sheet panels tends to relate to the size of sheets available (normally 1.5 m width maximum), and the weight of units when assembled. Panels at the Bronx Centre, which were mainly 3.45 m wide × 0.75 m, 1.5 m and 1.35 m high, made near maximum use of available rolled sheet sizes. Some curved panels were also used on the projecting staircase enclosures 3.6 m high × 0.862 m wide (see Fig. 5.13). Because of cost, plasterboard linings were selected for this project and it is interesting to note that

155

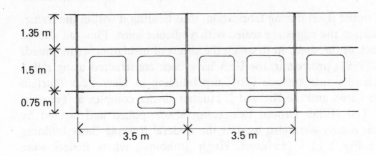

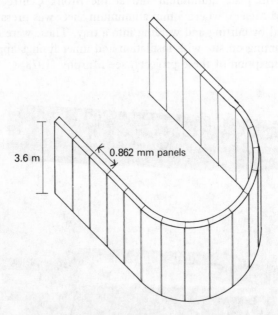

Fig. 5.13 Dimensions of panels used at the Bronx Centre, New York (architects: Richard Meier).

the curved corners to the windows had to be made good in plaster on the inside face.

Latest (1981) projects in the USA include 535 Madison Avenue office, New York (see Fig. 5.14) (architect: Edward Larrabee Barnes; manufacturers: Flour City), and the Johnson and Johnson building, New Brunswick, NJ (architect: I. M. Pei; curtain walling by Trio Industries). Figure 5.15 shows a detail from the Johnson and Johnson building which incorporates a gutter system at the base of the panels to collect any water which may penetrate the sealant (usually silicone) joint system. Weepholes are also provided to discharge the

Fig. 5.14 535 Madison Avenue, New York (architects: Edward Larrabee Barnes).

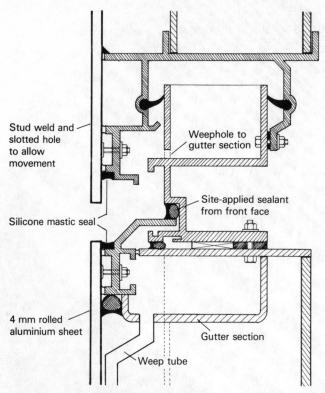

Stud weld and
slotted hole
to allow
movement

Weephole to
gutter section

Site-applied sealant
from front face

Silicone mastic seal

4 mm rolled
aluminium sheet

Gutter section

Weep tube

Fig. 5.15 Horizontal joint detail from Johnson and Johnson building, New Brunswick, USA (architects: I. M. Pei).

water to the outside face. Also note the method of 'floating' the aluminium sheet on to the panel framework, using studs welded on to the sheet with slotted holes to permit thermal movement.

European examples of rolled sheet panel construction would include the Hochhaus Dresdner Bank in Frankfurt (see Fig. 5.16). (Panels by Josef Gartner; architects: Becker, Becker and Partners.) Here the panels consist of 2.5 mm aluminium rolled sheet outer skin, which is deep drawn into a tray and screwed to an aluminium carrier system. Figure 5.17 shows the junction between two panels where the carrier is in four sections forming the outer and inner parts of the assembly. The aluminium skin is fixed to the outer section of the carrier, which is separated from the inner section by a thermal break. The inner lining and insulation panel is fixed to the inner section of the carrier, which in turn is bolted back to the main structural framing. For further details see Brookes and Ward (1981) Part II.

Fig. 5.16 Hochhaus Dresdner Bank, Frankfurt.

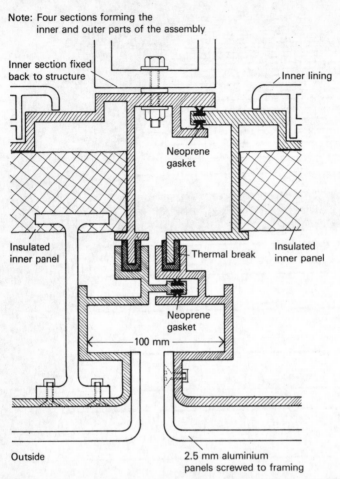

Note: Four sections forming the
      inner and outer parts of the assembly

Inner section fixed
back to structure

Inner lining

Neoprene
gasket

Insulated
inner panel

Thermal break

Insulated
inner panel

Neoprene
gasket

100 mm

Outside

2.5 mm aluminium
panels screwed to framing

Fig. 5.17 Plan of joint between panels at Hochhaus Dresdner Bank, Frankfurt (architects: Becker, Becker and Partners).

Box-type panels

This type of panel is fabricated from two metal skins with insulation inside to form the box where both faces of the box panel serve as the finished exterior or interior surfaces. The insulation can be foamed between the two metal skins or, in some cases, assembled *in situ* with the insulation and inner lining pop-riveted on-site. The thickness of the metal used will depend upon the size of the panel and whether the insulation core can be considered to add to the panel stiffness. Normal gauge of metal used for box-type panels is 1.5–2 mm thick. Panels often incorporate a thermal break where the two pans meet.

Box-type panels (see Fig. 5.18) were used at the Sainsbury Centre, University of East Anglia (architects: Foster Associates), where the 1800 mm × 1200 mm

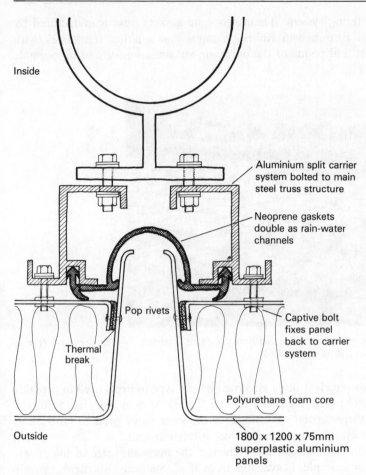

Fig. 5.18 Joints between panels at Sainsbury Centre (architects: Foster Associates).

panels were manufactured using vacuum-forming techniques, using a special alloy patented by the British Aluminium Company. This 'supral' alloy has the advantage over conventional aluminium alloy in that it will flow or 'run' at the right temperature and can be extended to ten times its original length. Using this alloy, panels can be formed into intricate shapes in one operation. However, the process of manufacture is slow and costly and some technical difficulties were at first experienced in forming the corners of the panels. Each outer tray is filled with 100 mm phenelux foam (curved decorative sections being filled with polystyrene) and the inner skins are then pushed into the outer trays and pop-riveted together through a small section of phenolic foam core, which forms the thermal break at the edge of the panel. Thermal transmission of the panels is $U = 0.47$ W/m² °C.

The aim was to produce a U-shaped one-piece continuous ladder gasket which fitted into an aluminium carrier system forming not only the main seal, but also the guttering system. These neoprene gaskets were manufactured by the Leyland and Birmingham Rubber Company as a lattice framework with two-way joints at mid-points of the overhang vulcanised on-site using portable equipment (see Fig. 5.19).

Fig. 5.19   Lattice gaskets used at Sainsbury Centre (courtesy of The Leyland & Birmingham Rubber Co. Ltd).

The size of box panels is often governed by the type of press used to produce the box tray. Steel panels produced for the 'Patera' system (see Fig. 5.20) are stamped out in three separate pressings for the same panel prior to fabrication into a composite unit using a mineral wool insulation core.

The types of metal used can also influence the maximum size of the panel. Stainless steel, for example, is available from BSC (Stainless) Sheffield, in coils up to 1520 mm wide. Similarly, zero carbon flattened steel, necessary for the manufacture of vitreous enamelled panels, is available in widths up to 1520 mm. Consequently, the size of vitreous enamelled panels is normally restricted in size to 2950 mm × 1450 mm allowing for a flange dimension. Panels can, of course, be assembled into a larger assembly using supporting framing; for example, façade units 3.86 m wide × 4.42 m high at Burne House Telecommunications Centre, London, were made up from panels less than 1 m wide mounted into a steel channel cladding frame. The construction incorporates a vapour barrier and a conventional inner lining.

Proprietary box-type panels

As well as 'one-off' designs for specific projects, a number of proprietary panels systems are marketed in the UK using box-type construction with both steel and aluminium metal skins, some of which are described below.

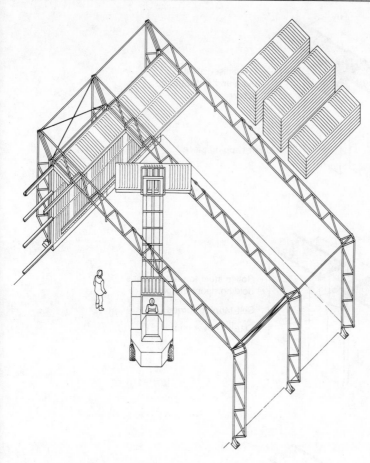

Fig. 5.20 'Patera' building systems using panels 3.6 m × 1.2 m (courtesy of Patera Products Ltd).

'Perfrisa' panels

Composite box-type panels using two skins of 0.5 mm thick galvanised steel with a foamed polyurethane core of average density 40 kg/m³ are marketed by Briggs Amasco as 'Perfrisa' panels. Joints between panels are formed by a butt joint neoprene gasket with a joint-capping piece in matching finish with the panels (see Fig. 5.21(a)). Width of panel 900 mm, thickness 30–100 mm, lengths up to 12 m.

'Formawall' panels

Steel laminate panels produced by H. H. Robertson (UK) Ltd with a foamed polyurethane core of average density 41.6 kg/m³. Embossed versacor exterior finish.

163

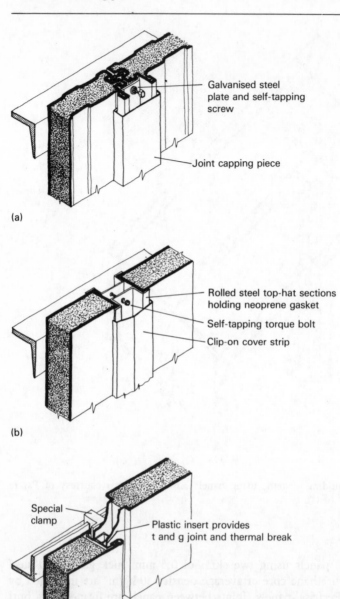

(a)

Galvanised steel
plate and self-tapping
screw

Joint capping piece

(b)

Rolled steel top-hat sections
holding neoprene gasket

Self-tapping torque bolt

Clip-on cover strip

(c)

Special
clamp

Plastic insert provides
t and g joint and thermal break

Fig. 5.21 Examples of proprietary box-type panel joints: (a) Briggs Amasco 'Perfrisa';
(b) Booth-Murie 'Simplan 1200' (c) Hunter Douglas 'Luxalon'.

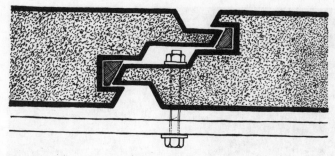

Fig. 5.22   H. H. Robertson 'Formawall' panel.

Overlap joint incorporates a two-stage jointing sealant. Panel width 600–900 mm, thickness 50 mm, lengths up to 10 m (see Fig. 5.22).

'Simplan 1200'

The panels comprising a lamination of two skins of 22 g plastic-coated steel with a Styrofoam 1B core, are produced by Bradley Laminates Ltd, for Booth-Murie Ltd. Joints between panels are formed using a top-hat rolled steel support with a clip-on matching joint cover strip (see Fig. 5.21b).

'Luxalon' panels

Aluminium panels with foamed polyurethane cores are supplied by Hunter Douglas as 'Luxalon' panels. Tongue and groove joints are used between panels with special clamps and sealing gasket fixing the panels back to the cladding rail at this joint (See Fig. 5.21). Plastic edging pieces are incorporated between the aluminium skins to prevent cold bridging.

Crawford 324 cladding

Originally developed as an overhead door section by Crawford Doors, these panels are now available in widths between 500 and 750 mm and lengths up to 12 m.

The panels are produced on a continuous lamination process with a foamed polyurethane core. Finishes are PVF2 coach-painted, aluzinc-coated steel finish and stucco-embossed aluminium. Vertical joints between panels are formed using neoprene gaskets.

'Unishield Snaplap'

Cape Universal claddings offer this range of insulated cladding panels comprising profiled steel or aluminium with a polyisocyanurate foam core and flat or profiled steel or aluminium lining sheets.

Fig. 5.23 'Metecno' patent fixing device (courtesy of Metecno (UK) Ltd).

'Metecno' panels

Metecno (UK) Ltd offer a range of composite insulated cladding and decking panels, all of which utilise two-colour-coated steel sheets with polyisocyanurate insulation. Their 'Glamet' panels are primarily designed as roof panels. 'Monowall' and 'Somatherm' panels are designed as wall panels, the former using exposed fixings through the panel to the structure, the latter using concealed fixings with a patent fixing clip (see Fig. 5.23).

Several Russian examples of box-type composite panels and their joints are shown in Fig. 5.24. Experience in the use of composite panels in New Zealand is also reported by Sharman and Duncan (1980).

In the same way as some allowance must be made for thermal expansion using sheet metals, similarly for box-type panels consideration must be made for possible thermal movement, particularly when using aluminium. Simple calculation shows that if the exterior panel temperature varies by 20 °C, then for a 1200 mm wide panel with a steel skin (coefficient of linear thermal expansion approximately 12×10^{-6} °C) the width will vary by 1 mm. An aluminium skin would

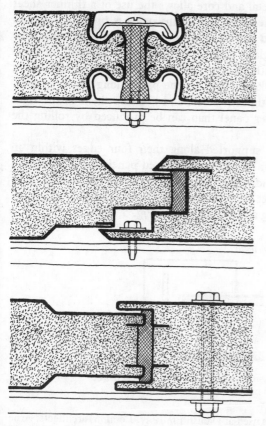

Fig. 5.24 Examples of joints between composite units developed in the Soviet Union.

move twice this amount. Thermal movement is normally allowed for at the joint and if an overlap H-shaped aluminium extrusion is used (similar to that shown in Fig. 5.21), then the legs of the H-section should be long enough to accommodate this movement. It is not good practice to 'gun in' a sealant into these sections to provide a final seal as this can be squeezed out on to the face of the panel due to the thermal movement (Sharman and Duncan, 1980). Vertical movement of the panels must also be allowed for in the design of any top and bottom fixings.

Laminated panels

This type of panel consists of two metal skins and layer, or layers, of insulation which are glued together under pressure to produce a strong non-loadbearing panel capable of spanning between secondary framing. Figure 5.9(c) shows a typical 'sandwich' or 'laminated' panel assembly. One method of production of laminated panels is shown in Fig. 5.6.

The integral strength of the metal and core allows the use of a thinner sheet of between 1.2–2.0 mm. Often the outer skin of the panel is press braked and shaped prior to being pressed and the edges of the panel reinforced with neoprene or timber, or even foamed glass, edging pieces. It is not unusual for these sandwich panels to be mounted within a steel or aluminium carrier system, using a capping piece and neoprene gasket to support the panel along its four edges.

The process of pressing these thinner sheets and bonding them to the rigid insulation usually provides a flatter panel than can be produced by rolling the sheet material.

Laminated panels are usually supported along their four edges within an aluminium or steel carrier system; for example, pressed panels using 64 mm of mineral fibre insulation board sandwiched between two layers of 16 gauge aluminium on 6 mm of asbestos sheet were used at the Danish Embassy, London (architects: Arne Jacobsen Dissing and Weitling) (see Fig. 5.25).

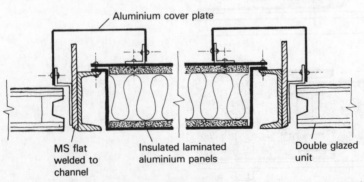

Aluminium cover plate

MS flat
welded to
channel

Insulated laminated
aluminium panels

Double glazed
unit

Fig. 5.25 Plan of laminated panel as used at Danish Embassy, London (architects: Arne Jacobsen, Dissing and Weitling).

Laminated sheets can be manufactured as thin infill panelling, 6–10 mm thick, such as 'Alucobond', manufactured by Swiss Aluminium Ltd, which consists of two sheets of aluminium (Peralumen NS 41) each 0.5 mm thick bonded to a low-density polyethylene core. The exceptional flatness and stiffness of these thin panels makes them ideal for use with glazing techniques. For example,

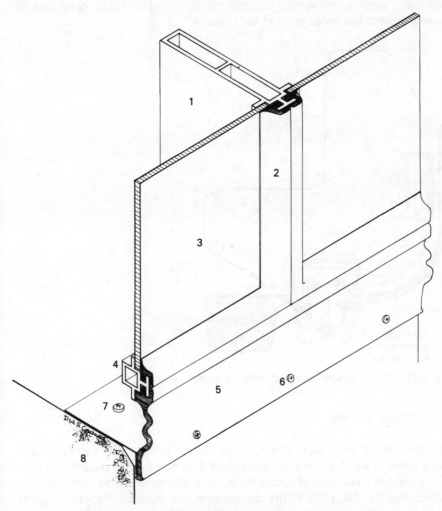

Fig. 5.26 Alucobond sheets at Winwick Quay, Warrington (courtesy of D. Cousans). (1) 150 mm × 25 mm extruded aluminium cladding mullion spanning 4800 mm vertically. (2) Preformed continuous neoprene gasket. (3) 6 mm anodic silver finished Alucobond. (4) 25 mm × 25 mm extruded aluminium horizontal cladding rail spanning 1250 mm between mullions. (5) Preformed neoprene tolerance strip. (6) Self-tapping screws fixing neoprene back aluminium cill. (7) Aluminium cill screwed down to concrete slab (8) 200 mm power-floated reinforced concrete slab

169

2.4 m × 1.25 m panels at Winwick Quay factory, Warrington (architects: Nicholas Grimshaw Partnership), are supported by a 150 × 25 mm extruded aluminium presslock system by Modern Art Glass (see Fig. 5.26). For a detailed study of this construction see Brookes and Ward (1981) Part II.

It is interesting to note that this principle of fixing formed panels back to a carrier system using neoprene gaskets was suggested by Jean Prouvé in his early drawings, using a lightweight concrete carrier (see Fig. 5.27). Note also the curved thinner laminated sheet at the corners.

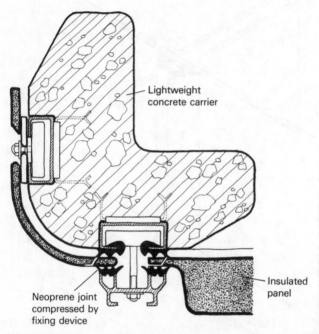

Fig. 5.27 Prouvé system using lightweight concrete carrier.

Rain screen panels

This last type of panel is, in effect, a combination of the rolled sheet and laminated panel in which a flat aluminium sheet 4–6 mm thick is mounted in front of a laminated panel itself designed for weather resistance with a ventilated cavity between the two parts of the construction. As the name 'screen' suggests, these panels are only a first-stage barrier. The panels behind provide the thermal and acoustic performance and can be mounted into a carrier system or fixed to secondary framing in the same way as previously described. Figure 5.9(d) shows a typical example of 'rain screen' construction with a thermal break between the inner and outer part of the carrier system. The joints between the rain screen panel should be 10 mm or more to allow for any thermal movement, and it is also advised that the fixing of the outer sheets to the carrier system should also allow for movement. The gauge of the plate panel must also be such to avoid rippling and distortion of the sheet (in aluminium 4–6 mm). For a further discussion of 'rain screen' and pressure-equalised wall design, see Architectural Aluminium Manufacturers Association booklet (1971),and the following chapter on curtain walling. This system of construction was used at the Umschlags AG office building in Basel (see Fig. 5.28), (architects: Wetterwald and Wenger), where 1651 mm wide × 2060 mm high decorative aluminium panels were deep drawn by Schmidlin and in effect 'hooked' on to the building, with an air gap of 20–30 mm provided between the outer panel and the insulation to ensure ventilation of the rain screen principle. For further details see Brookes and Ward (1981) Part II. Figure 5.29 shows a UK example of a rain screen by Crittall Construction, again showing the air gap, the method of clipping the rain screen to the carrier and the thermal break.

The size of the panel is only limited by the maximum size of the sheet metal panel and its ability to span between supports. However, it must be remembered that the outside face of the inner laminated panel must also be waterproof and this may limit the size of the overall assembly if joints in this panel are to be avoided.

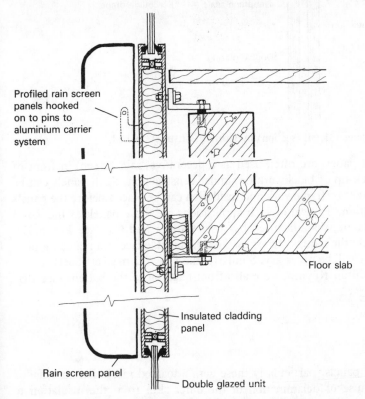

Profiled rain screen panels hooked on to pins to aluminium carrier system

Floor slab

Insulated cladding panel

Rain screen panel

Double glazed unit

Fig. 5.28 Section of panels used at Umschlags AG office building, Basel (architects: Wetterwald and Wenger).

171

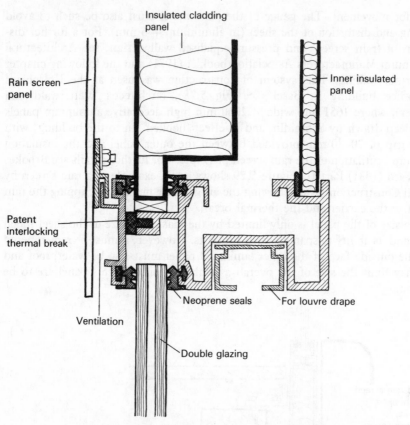

Fig. 5.29 Rain screen detail (section) by Crittall Construction Ltd.

Small formed panels are often used as a decorative 'rain screen' in front of conventional back-up of blockwork or similar construction. Such panels can be mounted on battens or framework and insulation can be placed before the panels are fixed in position. Typical of such applications are those panels at the Royal Library, The Hague, manufactured by Josef Gartner and Co. (see Fig. 5.31). Using this method the fixings are exposed on the outside face and matching plastic capping pieces will be necessary. Similarly, the 1 m × 2 m steel panels at Kiln Farm factory, Milton Keynes, were also front-fixed on to the battens (see Fig. 5.30).

Delamination

Some composite panels, particularly those with a foamed insulation core, failed in the past because of delamination of the outer skin from the insulation to which they were bonded. This, in turn, reduced the spanning characteristics of the panel, since the materials no longer acted in a composite fashion. Tests car-

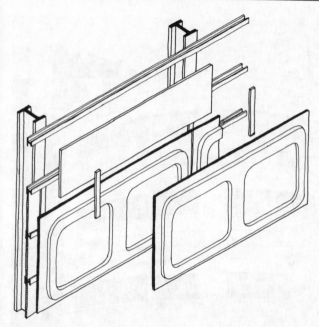

Fig. 5.30 Steel panels used at Milton Keynes factory, Kiln Farm (architects: M.K.D.C.).

ried out by the BRE by Dr R. Thorogood (1979) showed panels which were subject to this phenomenon and suggested steps to be taken to prevent it. Delamination is caused by the sun heating up the outer skin of the panel which consequently expands, while the inner skin remains at a low temperature due to the insulation. An unrestrained panel will bow outwards to accommodate this extension and there will be relatively little stress set up between the outer skin and the core. However, if such a panel is fixed to a structure so that its ability to bow is limited by the fixings, then the stress set up at the interface of the skin and the core will be considerably greater and delamination is likely to occur. The stresses can be reduced if the edges of the panel are free to bend as the panel bows out and are not restrained by the adjacent panels or the method of fixing. Other factors in design can reduce the effect of this thermal movement:

1. Use light colours or reflective colours on the outer skin to reduce the heat gain on the skin.
2. The size of the panel should be taken into consideration. Large panels will deflect more than small ones.
3. Fixings in the centre of panels should be avoided.
4. The adhesive and type of insulation core should be selected to take account of stresses set up by thermal movement.
5. If the inner skin has a higher coefficient of expansion than the outer (i.e. aluminium inner skin/steel outer skin), then the effect of thermal movement will be reduced.

Fig. 5.31 Panels at the Royal Library, The Hague (courtesy of Josef Gartner and Co.).

Considerable research has been carried out by reputable manufacturers into the selection of adhesives, insulation cores and specifications of their use. With careful design the issue of delamination can be resolved.

Adhesives

Bearing in mind the need to avoid delamination, the architect should seek advice from the manufacturer on the best type of adhesive related to the possible stresses that may be set up between the laminations and requirements for heat resistance. Lap shear strength up to 4000 psi is possible with some adhesives. The relative costs of the different adhesives may not be significant related to the total cost of the panel. There are three types of adhesive in widespread use for the production of laminated sandwich panels:

1. Neoprene contact adhesives.
2. One- and two-part polyurethanes.
3. One- and two-part epoxies.

It is sometimes difficult to bond mill-finished aluminium or galvanised steel due to the oxide layer on the surface which must be removed or strengthened chemi-

cally. Although special polyurethanes are available, the problem is better solved
by prior application of a thin coat of acid etch primer.

Insulation cores

Different types and thickness of sheet materials and foams can be used for the
insulation cores. These are (in order of expense):

mineral wool
honeycomb paper core
bead polystyrene rigid sheet
IB polystyrene rigid sheet
polyurethane foam (polyisocyanurate is a modified form of polyurethane to
improve fire retardancy).

Polystyrene sheet, which is produced by heating up polystyrene granules and
fusing them together with a combination of steam and pressing, is cheaper in
material cost than polyurethane foam (at 1981 prices approx. £600/tonne, against
£1000/tonne for polyurethane). However, polyurethane gives better insulation
than polystyrene (25 mm thick polyurethane has the same insulation value as
40 mm thick polystyrene, see Fig. 5.32) and it is easier to manufacture. Most
manufacturers of box-type proprietary panels prefer to use polyurethane or at

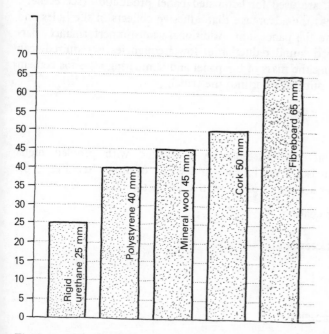

Fig. 5.32 Relative insulation performance of different core materials.

175

least its modified version, polyisocyanurate, which is used because of its fire retardancy.

The use of any particular type or thickness of core depends upon the stiffness required of the whole panel and the requirements for thermal and acoustic performance. In general for foamed materials, the higher the density the stiffer the panel, and the lower the density the ·better the insulation value. Note that the foam contains freon gas, which is the major insulator.

Polyurethane and polyisocyanurate foams can be foamed in place during production, either by:

- vertical pouring
- horizontal pouring or
- continuous lamination

Becker (1968) gives more details of methods of foam in place production and other detailed considerations for sandwich panel design. Profiled sheets of metal with polyisocyanurate backing are often produced on a continuous lamination process (see Fig. 5.33). Surfactants are necessary to ensure a closed cell and to maintain the quality of the foam.

·When manufacturing metal sheets in conjunction with an insulation core the effect of electrostatic charging (triboelectrics), when handling the sheets, cannot be ignored.

Mineral wool and honeycomb paper core, which normally contain polystyrene inserts within the core, are used for laminated panel production (see earlier). The honeycomb core has the advantage that adhesive collects in the holes and offers good adherence to the panel skin. Additional acoustic performance, particularly where improved sound reduction at low frequencies is required, can be obtained by increasing the mass of the panel and laminating asbestos cement sheet and high-density mineral wool into the panel.

Finishes

As well as the organic coatings normally associated with profiled metal claddings, such as Plastisol PVC finishes and PVF^2 coatings (see Fig. 5.6), manufacturers will offer a number of alternative finishes such as:

- electrostatic powder coating
- anodising
- thin premium paint coatings
- vitreous enamelling
- stainless steel

Electrostatic powder coating

Powder coating is the application of thermo-hardening polyester/polyurethane powders to conductive materials, with subsequent fusion and hardening in a hot

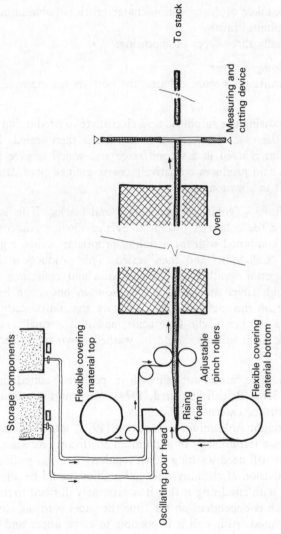

Fig. 5.33 Diagram of continuous lamination process.

air oven. This process has to be carried out in the factory and it is, therefore, necessary to coat matching flashings and trims. Cured coating thickness should not be less than 75 μm.

Anodising

Advantage can be taken of the oxidation characteristics of aluminium to provide an anodised aluminium finish.
There are essentially three types of anodising:

(a) *Natural anodising* – silver;
(b) *Two-stage anodising* – bronze colours (the best-known example in the UK is 'Anolok').

Both types of anodising use sulphuric acid electrolyte to produce an initial silver anodic film. In the case of silver anodising this is then sealed. In two-stage anodising, the film is dyed in a second stage and sealed to give the required shade. Sulphuric acid produces a relatively coarse-grained pore structure which is not as resistant to abrasion as:

(c) *Integral anodising* – (golds, bronzes, greys and blacks). This is a one-stage process where the colour is produced by the alloying constituents in the parent metal combined with the action of proprietary acids, e.g. 'Kalcolor,' 'Duranodic', 'Calonodic' and then sealed. This produces a dense anodic film with superior weathering characteristics and resistance to abrasion. Thus, although silver anodising is produced in one stage by the action of electrolyte on the metal, it does not have the film density of the true integral using sulphosalicylic type acids, and it is normally recommended that this type of anodising should be washed down more frequently than the other types.

Anodising should be carried out using alloys specifically suited for the process according to BS 3987 (British Standard, 1974). Minimum required anodic film thickness is 25 μm for external applications.

European Wrought Aluminium Association (1978) specifications for anodising types includes a terminology of aluminium anodising procedures. Anodised aluminium panels will need washing down regularly to avoid pitting of the surface and thus provision of cleaning rails and cradles should be allowed for.

One difficulty with anodising is that it is extremely difficult to match colours of anodising which is dependent on the time the panel is in the electrolyte and the type of alloy used. Although it is possible to agree upper and lower limits of colour variation with the manufacturer, some variation must inevitably be accepted, depending upon the degree of quality control in the factory.

Thin premium paint coatings

It is perhaps this difficulty of maintaining anodising quality that has led to some

American architects expressing a preference for more recent paint finishes, such as fluoropolymer coatings (e.g. 'Duranar' from PPG Industries) or acrylic finishes.

These premium, thin (20 μm) paint films are dependent for their performance on the type of substrate used and, as with all organic coating, long-term durability will be affected by the type of metal pretreatment used.

In addition to hot-dipped galvanising, i.e. a zinc finish, hot-dipped aluminised steel is also available. Although slightly more expensive than galvanising. this offers better corrosion resistance and can also be left uncoated.

Vitreous enamelling

Vitreous enamelling is normally associated with steel panels because it is difficult to ensure proper adherence of the enamel to aluminium sheeting. The zero carbon flattened steel necessary for the manufacture of vitreous enamelled panels is available in widths up to 1520 mm which can restrict the size of the finished panel.

Stainless steel

Stainless steel can also be used for external cladding. For laminate sheets in which the integral strength of the core allows the use of thinner gauge metal skin, the cost of stainless steel may not be significantly more than the equivalent stiffness gauge of aluminium with a hard anodic anodising. The surface finish of stainless steel can vary from a matt descaled finish to a bright, highly polished finish. The choice depends on the use and the cleaning technique to be applied. Number 4 dull polished finish, which is not highly reflective, is suitable for most architectural applications, since it combines ease of cleaning with uniformity of appearance.

References

Architectural Aluminium Manufacturers' Association (1971) *Aluminium Curtain Walls. Rain Screen Principle and Pressure-Equalised Wall Design – Design Details of Three Recent Buildings*, AAMA: Chicago.

Architectural Design (1963) 'The work of Jean Prouvé', *Architectural Design*, Nov. 1963, 511–25.

Becker, W. E. (1968) *U.S. Sandwich Panel Manufacturing Marketing Guide*, Technomic: Stamford, Conn. USA.

British Standard (1974) *Anodic oxide coatings on wrought aluminium for external architectural applications*, BS 3987.

Brookes, A. J. (1980) 'Products in practice – claddings. 2. Metal composite claddings', *Architects' Journal*, 5.11.1980, 905–14.

Brookes, A. J. and Ward, M. (1981) 'The art of construction – sheet metal claddings, Part I "The range of systems"', *Architects' Journal*, 8.7.1981, 77–85. 'Part II "Case studies"', *Architects' Journal*, 15.7.1981, 121–6.

European Wrought Aluminium Association (1978) *Specification for the Quality Sign for Anodic Oxidation Coatings on Wrought Aluminium for Architectural Purposes*, EWAA: June, 1978.

Huber, B. and Steinegger, J. C. (1971) *Jean Prouvé*, Les Editions d'Architecture, Artemis: Zurich.

Murphy, J. (1978) 'Skin deep, technics for external wall panels', *Progressive Architecture*, vol. 2 (1978), 83–91.

Sebestyen, C. (1977) 'External walls design principles', *Lightweight Building Construction*, Ch. 3, Wiley: New York.

Sharman W. R. and Duncan, J. R. (1980) 'Building materials usage in primary processing industry buildings – sandwich panels', Branz Technical Paper, p. 30 Oct. 1980, pp. 20–23.

Thorogood, R. (1979) *Metal Skinned Sandwich Panels for External Walls*, BRE CP6/79.

Chapter 6

Curtain walling

Definition

'Curtain walling' may be defined as being non-loadbearing walls, usually suspended in front of a structural frame; their own deadweight and wind loadings being transferred to the structural frame through anchorage points. Usually they consist of a rectangular grid of vertical or horizontal framing with infill panels of glass or some other lightweight panel; but that is not always so for the term 'curtain walling' encompasses a wide variety of systems.

(a) Patent glazing.
(b) Metal window section as framing.
(c) Pressed or extruded metal box framing.
(d) Suspended glass assemblies.

There are a number of proprietary systems available for each of these types.

Patent glazing

Nineteenth-century Victorian glasshouses gave many opportunities for the development of dry assembly systems of glass and metal. Many of these are shown by Hix (1974) in his excellent historical study of glasshouse construction. Joseph Paxton's Crystal Palace had wooden glazing bars made on-site by sophisticated milling machines, but by the time it was moved to Sydenham it was largely rebuilt using metal glazing bars and a puttyless glazing system, the recognised advantage of which was illustrated by the abundance of patents taken out at that time (hence patent glazing). Sections of the nineteenth-century patent glazing bars are shown in Guedes (1979). It was the necessity to provide good natural lighting in factories, using north light roof construction in the 1920s and 1930s, which really promoted the commercial development of the large number of types of patent glazing sections used today. Modern patent glazing systems for both inclined and vertical applications are shown in Patent Glazing Conference publications (1980).

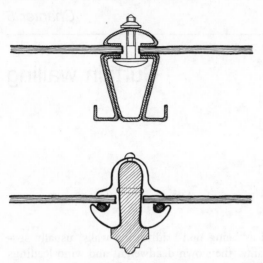

Fig. 6.1 Sections of nineteenth-century glazing bars (from Guedes, 1979).

Traditionally the patent glazing techniques assumed an inclined plane of glass supported on two edges by the 'table' of the glazing bars with the 'stalk' of the bar projecting outwards. In this way the glass was pressing down on to the glazing bead by its own weight, and gravity held it in place (on two edges) using a spring clip. The glass was lapped on its other edges with an open joint. Gradually patent glazing began to be used for vertical applications and it was then necessary to prevent the glass sliding down the sections by restraining it on all four edges.

There are two forms of patent glazing (see Fig. 6.2):

(a) Traditional, with the glazing bar projecting outside;
(b) Inverted, with the glazing bar projecting inside.

Types of patent glazing are also shown in Patent Glazing Conference (1978). Although at first sight the choice of 'traditional' or 'inverted' method might be seen as purely an aesthetic decision, in fact it stems from a pragmatic approach to the design of this type of construction. In the traditional method the clip is used to push down the glass on to the glazing bead with the table of the glazing bar fixed to the structure with fixing shoes. This method depends upon the spring of the clip pushing against the sealing cord. Any penetration of water would be collected in the inner water channel which also copes with condensation inside.

To exert a more positive pressure on the seals such as neoprene it was necessary to invert the section to allow a screw cap fixed from the outside, with a clip-on extruded cover providing no visible fixing screws. The inverted use of patent glazing has recently found favour as the weathering skin to solar collectors supporting the underside of the solar panel.

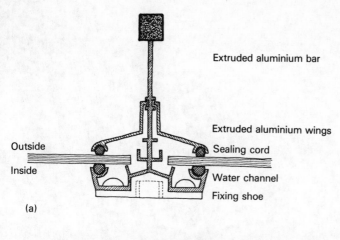

Extruded aluminium bar

Extruded aluminium wings

Outside

Sealing cord

Inside

Water channel

Fixing shoe

(a)

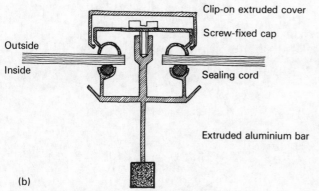

Clip-on extruded cover

Screw-fixed cap

Outside

Inside

Sealing cord

Extruded aluminium bar

(b)

Fig. 6.2   Two forms of patent glazing: (a) traditional; (b) inverted.

Use of patent glazing

Crawford (1974) describes the lack of expertise during the last decade in handling details of junctions required beyond those of simple geometric planes of patent glazing. He cites the first appreciative use of these techniques by James Stirling with his former partner James Gowan. Their Leicester University Engineering building (1959–63) exploited the potential of patent glazing, which has since become a distinctive feature of Stirling's architectural style. Patent glazing has been used in other building types during the 1970s in schools, offices and even private homes. The GLC's Pimlico school (see Fig. 6.3) completed in 1970 is a good example of patent glazing used for total fenestration. It has been

Following pages:

Fig. 6.3   GLC Pimlico school (courtesy of Gareth Abbott).

Fig. 6.4   Schreiber furniture factory, Runcorn (courtesy of Brock, Carmichael Associates).

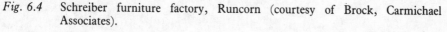

exploited in flexible industrial accommodation units giving plenty of natural lighting, while enabling the tenants to change any glazing to meet user requirements.

The Schreiber furniture factory, Runcorn (architects: Brock, Carmichael Associates) has recently been completed using patent glazing. The roof of the factory is designed as a re-entrant glass-sided metal decking lid over the plastic-coated metal wall cladding (see Fig. 6.4). The re-entrant angle of the glazing reduces solar gain and glare while the large areas of glazing provide daylighting and ensure continuous visual contact with the outside world. Liverpool Playhouse Theatre (architects: Hall, O'Donahue and Wilson) (see Fig. 6.5) also uses a rolled steel glazing bar section with a snap-on cap in extruded unplasticised PVC (see Fig. 6.6).

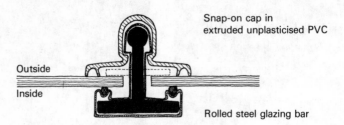

Snap-on cap in extruded unplasticised PVC

Outside

Inside

Rolled steel glazing bar

Fig. 6.6   Vertical joint as used at Liverpool Playhouse Theatre (architects: Hall, O'Donahue and Wilson).

With the market changing from the conventional use of glazing in the sloped factory roof to use as a popular vertical cladding, greater attention is now paid to external finish and fixings with many sections being available within manufacturers' systems. The development of the four-edge support system allows the opportunity of wider glazing bay modules. (Traditionally patent glazing bars were required to be at 600 mm intervals where the glass was only supported along its two long edges.) The introduction of transomes also allows changes from glass to panels and the inclusion of ventilators, etc.

British Standard (1977) BS 5516, the code of practice for patent glazing, includes design recommendations for two-edge supported systems, as well as systems where the glass is secured on all four edges. An appendix in the British Standard gives the working methods and tables necessary to determine patent glazing bar sectional properties from first principles. Another useful guide is that published as part of the *Architects' Journal* 'Products in Practice' series (3.12.1980), in which drawing board data includes methods of design, glazing bar materials, double glazing and application details (see Fig. 6.7).

Patent glazing bars are listed as available in the following materials:

- extruded aluminium alloy sections to BS 1474

Fig. 6.5   Liverpool Playhouse Theatre (architects: Hall, O'Donahue and Wilson).

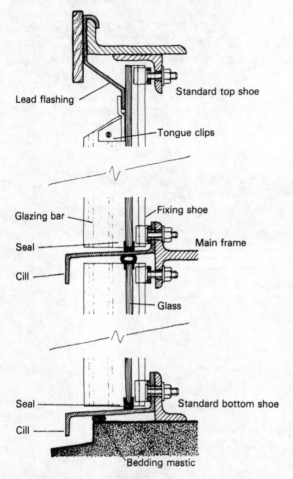

Fig. 6.7 Patent glazing application details.

- mild steel bar to BS 18 (tensile strength not less than 360 N/mm²) either as:
  (a) hot-dipped galvanised finish;
  (b) lead-clothed steel; or
  (c) extruded PVC sheathed steel.

Metal box framing

The term 'curtain walling' is most commonly associated with a rectangular grid of vertical and horizontal frame members, introduced from America during the 1950s mainly for use in high-rise office buildings (see Hunt, 1958). Two buildings in particular helped the popular aesthetic approval of the framed curtain wall: the United Nations Secretariat (Harrison and others, 1947–50) and Lever House (Skidmore, Owings and Merrill, 1952), both in New York. Important forerunners of these were buildings such as the Gropius factory at Alfeld (1911), the Bauhaus, Dessau (1925–26) and Le Corbusier's Maison Suisse at the Cité Université, Paris (1930–32).

There are two basic approaches to assembling a box-framed curtain wall (see Fig. 6.8). Either:

1. the component parts of the system are assembled on-site with panels being offered up to a frame (sometimes known as the 'stick' system); or

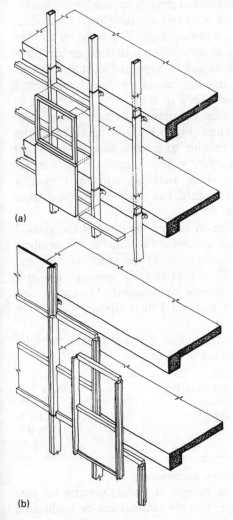

(a)

(b)

Fig. 6.8 Basic forms of curtain walling construction: (a) 'stick' system; (b) 'panel' system.

2. the panel system is bolted together, the panels themselves becoming the frame.

Both systems have the advantages associated with a high degree of prefabrication; the first method has more easily handled components but site construction time may be longer.

Typical spans

In both systems the window mullions are the principal members of the grid: horizontal members rarely form the support for curtain walls. Vertical members spanning from floor to floor must withstand axial stresses caused by self-weight and bending caused by wind loads, and it is in this direction that the mullion must have greatest stiffness and strength, a principle also illustrated by the 'fin' section of a patent glazing bar. The depth of the mullion is thus dependent upon its span and the area of glazing it is required to support (module spacing). Prouvé illustrated as early as the 1930s how the use of a range of proprietary sections could cope with a variety of spans (see Fig. 6.9).

It is interesting to reflect that some recent examples of curtain walling techniques, as illustrated by the Sainsbury Centre (Fig. 6.10), rely upon the glazing members being fixed back to the main framing to provide their stiffness and strength. Thus while the conventional curtain walling is intended to 'free up' the sheath wall from the main structure of the building, with more modern applications there is a tendency for the structural bay sizes to be related more strictly to the grid of the curtain walling.

The size of the curtain wall grid is determined by the costs of the vertical members, the section size being weighed alongside the number of members required. Proprietary systems offer a module size of between 760 mm and 1200 mm, and according to Elder (1977), where mullion spacings are over 1200 mm, glass costs and mullion sizes increase considerably. Maximum sizes of different types of glass are shown on p. 11 of Patent Glazing Conference (1978).

It is, therefore, interesting to observe a number of recent (1981) examples of curtain walling where the module sizes are given as:

Radio Chemical Centre, Cardiff (Percy Thomas Partnership)	0.6 and 1.2 m.
5 Ways Tower, Birmingham (PSA Midlands Region)	2.7 m.
Zuider Zee Nurseries, Toddington (Anthony Perella)	1.2 m
Bedford Midland Station (BR Board)	0.9
IBM Greenford (Foster Associates)	2.4 m.

Thus larger bay spacings than 1.2 m are not uncommon.

It may be that with the introduction of designs of glazing systems for particular projects rather than for general use, that the sections can be engineered for larger mullion spacings. Float and sheet glasses are now available for use with these larger grid dimensions. Information on maximum sizes normally

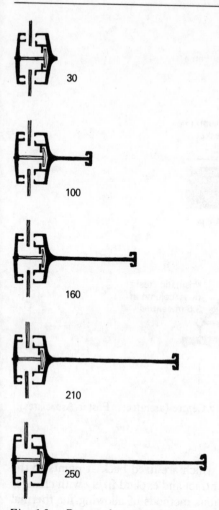

Fig. 6.9 Range of sections (depth) to cope with a variety of spans.

available for glasses used in curtain walling can be obtained from the various glass manufacturers, including Pilkington Bros., St Helens. British Standard 6262: 1982 *Code of practice glazing for buildings* also gives information on design considerations affecting spanning characteristics of different types of glass.

Joints and connections

The logic underlying the frequency at which prefabricated curtain walling elements are jointed together can be summarised in terms of manageability (both in transportation and in site handling) and reduction of movement per joint, particularly thermal, in the system and between the system and the supporting framework.

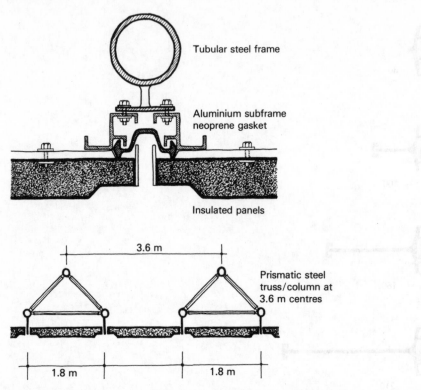

Fig. 6.10 Support system as used at Sainsbury Centre (architects: Foster Associates).

Joints to allow thermal movement

The framing members of the curtain wall which are fixed back at points to the supporting structure must be allowed to contract and expand freely with changes of temperature. Rostron (1964) shows various methods of allowing for thermal

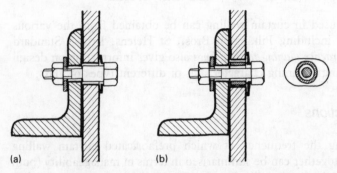

Fig. 6.11 Reduction of friction at sliding connections by using slotted holes and plastic washers and: (a) shoulder bolts; (b) sleeves and standard bolts (from Rostron, 1964).

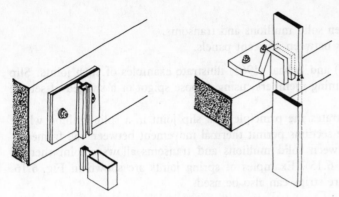

Fig. 6.12 Allowance for thermal movement in methods of fixing (from Rostron, 1964).

movement (see Figs 6.11 and 6.12) between the framing and structure using sliding joints. Reduction of friction at sliding connections is provided by slotted holes and plastic washers.

It is also essential to provide some kind of discontinuity in the frame itself. Frequent jointing within the frame will reduce the thermal movement per joint in the system and between the system and the main structure. There are essentially three types of such joints:

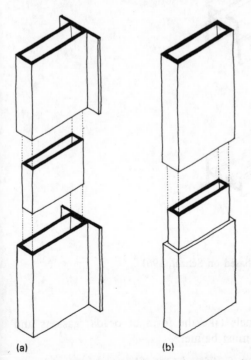

(a)   (b)

Fig. 6.13 Two types of slip joints in vertical framing members (based on Rostron, 1964). (a) Loose spigot or sleeve; (b) Swaged offset

1. *Slip joints*.
2. *Butt joints* between solid mullions and transoms.
3. *Spring connections* between adjacent panels.

Both Rostron (1964) and Schaal (1961) illustrate examples of such joints. Slip joints in vertical framing members, using a loose spigot or a swaged offset are shown in Fig. 6.13.

Figure 6.14 illustrates the principle of a slip joint in a split mullion where the male and female sections permit thermal movement between the frames.

Butt splicing between solid mullions and transoms allows a joint thermal movement (see Fig. 6.15). Examples of spring joints are shown in Fig. 6.16. Flexible metal closure strips can also be used.

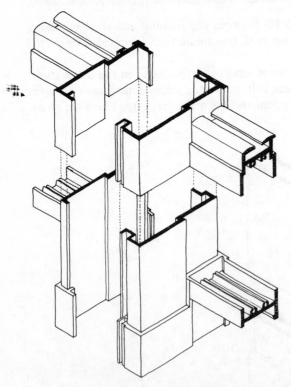

Fig. 6.14 Slip joints in split mullions (based on Schaal, 1961).

Weatherproof joints

Joints between frame and infill panels take the form of beads, gaskets and sealants; the following requirements must be met:

1. Joints should be wind- and rainproof (if inside of infill panel is sensitive to moisture, edges should be protected).

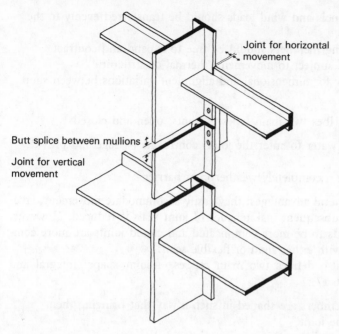

Joint for horizontal movement

Butt splice between mullions

Joint for vertical movement

Fig. 6.15 Butt joints between solid mullions and transoms (based on Schaal, 1961).

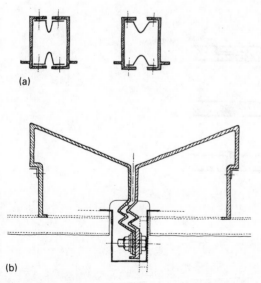

(a)

(b)

Fig. 6.16 Spring connections (based on Schaal, 1961): (a) flexible metal closures in the joints; (b) example of a spring joint.

195

2. Self-weight of panels and wind loads should be transferred evenly to the frame.
3. Panels and framing members should be free to expand and contract independently (if subject to movement; thermal or structural).
4. Joints must allow for dimensional and alignment variations between shop and site.

Rostron (1964) describes two main types of joints: open and closed:

• *Open joints* allow water to enter the joint, control its passage and provide drainage.
• *Closed joints* form a completely weatherproof barrier.

The former have several advantages; they easily accommodate movement, erection is quick, and subsequent maintenance of joint seals is reduced. However, the joint profile tends to be more complicated and closed joints are more commonly used sealed with either rigid or flexible seals.

Rostron (1964) also defines two main classes of joint shape: integral and accessory (see Fig. 6.17):

• *Integral joints*: members are shaped in such a way that bringing them together forms the joint.
• *Accessory joints*: require additional parts to form the joint.

Each of these joint shapes has three principal forms (see Fig. 6.17). The choice

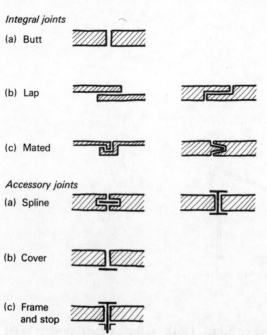

Fig. 6.17 Integral and accessory joints (based on Rostron, 1964).

of joint shape is determined by requirements for tolerance in assembly, movement, sequence of assembly, performance factors and aesthetics.

The component nature of curtain walling means there are many joints in the envelope. These joints, at frequent intervals, are necessary to enable components to be of manageable dimensions. Frequent jointing will also reduce the problem of thermal movement per joint. Recent years have seen the development of more sophisticated joints moving away from metal and mastic joints between panels towards patent neoprene gasket designs. Neoprene also helps to accommodate thermal movement between the panel and its framing.

Joints between glass and frame

When glass is the infilling panel the edge cover given to the panel at the joint has to be limited in order to avoid too great a temperature differential occurring between the edge and the exposed surface, which may lead to the glass breaking. Stroud, Foster and Harington (1976) (p. 170–1) recommend that the edge cover to the glass should be limited to 10 mm, although a dark-coloured frame will alleviate the problem of thermal stressing. A more detailed discussion of glass fracture is contained in T. A. Schwartz's paper to the Second International Conference on the Durability of Building Materials, 1981 (Frohnsdorff, 1981) in which he advises designers to consider the strength-degrading effects of long-term loads, environment and surface defects as part of their glass selection process. At the same conference Zarghamee and Schwartz reported on a study designed to discover causes for the loss of metal edge bands from insulating glass units during service (Frohnsdorff, 1981). Such studies have been carried out as a result of experience with glazing units that have failed either by seal fracture, or glass fracture, due to cyclic movement between the glass and the curtain wall; the most dramatic example is that of the Hancock Tower in Boston where it was necessary to stabilise the main frame in order to reduce the amount of movement.

Insulation and cold bridging

The thermal performance of the assembly is largely determined by the insulating properties of the infilling panel. The nature of the frame does, however, have some influence upon performance. If the frame is made of metal and is unprotected from the external environment, then it will set up a cold bridging pathway. The effect can be overcome by discontinuity in the framing members using a patent plastic thermal break (see Fig. 6.18). Examples of these have been given in the previous chapter on sheet metal claddings. In some systems the metal frame is continuously protected from external conditions by a neoprene gasket and in this way cold bridging is avoided. If the frame is constructed from timber members then no problems of cold bridging arise.

Fig. 6.18   Patent plastic thermal break

Fire resistance

A curtain wall has to be regarded as an unprotected area in relation to the transmission of fire to adjoining property. The extent to which an unprotected area is permitted by the fire provisions of the Building Regulations, or, if applicable, the London By-laws, is determined by the distance to the wall from the relevant boundary. A common method for reducing the unprotected area, which is acceptable under both sets of regulations, is to provide a non-combustible back-up wall, usually of masonry construction, 100 mm from the inner face of the infill panel. This approach does, however, invalidate certain advantages of a curtain wall installation, such as saving floor space and light loading of the primary structure.

The rain screen principle and pressure-equalised wall design

Twenty-five years ago the Norwegians initiated a scientific investigation into the mechanism of water leakage. Initially they were only concerned with the performance of casement windows, but their investigations subsequently led to a more thorough understanding of the behaviour of the wall itself. Birkeland (1962) published a treatise in which the principles of what was then referred to as the 'rain barrier' and its implications were discussed.

Following the studies of the Norwegians, scientists at the Canadian National Research Council's Division of Building Research Institute began similar investigations, and a year after the Norwegian publication, a small pamphlet entitled *Rain Penetration and its Control* by Garden (1963) had appeared. This publication is still considered to be a prime reference source in which the terms 'rain screen' and 'rain screen principle' are clearly defined.

A recent publication by the Architectural Aluminium Manufacturers' Association of America (1971) summarises the present position and makes the point that the terms 'rain screen principle' and 'pressure-equalised design', though closely related, are not strictly synonymous. The 'rain screen' is the outer skin or surface of a wall or wall elements backed by an air space and so designed that it shields the wall joints from wetting. As such it has been described in the previous chapter dealing with sheet metal cladding systems. The rain screen principle is a principle of design which describes how penetration of this screen by rain-water may be prevented. The use of pressure-equalised design is an essential part of this principle. Before discussing the application of this principle in detail, it is important to discuss how rain-water acts on the surface of a wall.

Forces acting to move water through an opening

None of the rain-water striking a metal and glass curtain wall is absorbed as it would be with masonry construction and a substantial film of water will flow down the surface. If wind is present, the water may also flow laterally or even upwards on parts of the building. The taller the building, the greater will be the accumulated flow over the lower parts of its walls. Lateral flow under wind pressure is greatest near the windward corners of the building and upward flow greatest near or at the top of the façade facing the wind. Lateral flow will also be concentrated at vertical irregularities in the wall surface, either projections or depressions, and these may often be joints. In general the flow of water at vertical joints is much greater than the average flow of water over the wall.

A number of forces then act to move the surface water through any available opening. All of these forces are illustrated schematically in Fig. 6.19. Probably

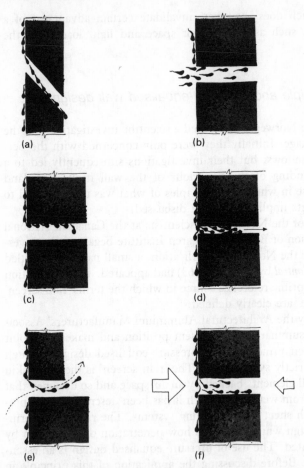

Fig. 6.19 Forces acting to move water through an opening: (a) gravity; (b) kinetic
energy; (c) surface tension; (d) capillary action; (e) air currents; (f) pressure
difference (based on AAMA, 1971).

the most familiar of these is the force of *gravity*, and appropriate methods of
counteracting this force are well known. Another force is *kinetic energy*. Rain-
drops may approach the wall surface with considerable velocity and their
momentum may carry them through any opening of sufficient size. Cover battens, splines or internal baffles can be used to prevent rain entry due to this type
of force. A third factor which contributes to leakage is *surface tension*, which
gives the water the ability to cling to and flow along soffit areas. The preven-
tative to this action is in the form of a drip at the outer edge of the overhang.
Fourthly, *capillary action* is likely to occur whenever the space separating two
wettable surfaces is small. The way to control water flow by capillarity is to
introduce a discontinuity or air gap in the joint of greater width than the capillary path. It is the next two forces caused by wind action which are the most

critical and most difficult to combat. *Air currents* may result from differences in wind pressure over the wall surface, or from convection within wall cavities. These may carry water into the wall. Also, if water is present on one side of an opening and the air pressure on that side is greater than that on the other side, the water will be moved through the opening, no matter how small, in the direction of the pressure drop. This *pressure* difference may be caused by even the gentlest of winds and causes most of the leakage at wall joints.

The conventional approach to combating the two latter forces was to attempt to eliminate all openings by using a tight seal, but the more effective and reliable approach is to eliminate the pressure differential across the opening. It is this approach that is known as the 'rain screen principle'. The essential features of the rain screen and pressure-equalised wall construction are shown in Fig. 6.20. Sketch (a) indicates how, with the larger pressure on the outside, water is normally drawn through the joint. Sketch (b) shows the condition where the pressures on two sides of the outer surface are made equal, thus preventing leakage by gravity, kinetic, surface tension or capillary action. Sketch (c) shows, in order to withstand the effects of air currents and wind pressure, how a continuous air space must be provided between the inner and outer skins of the construction.

The pressure-equalised wall consists essentially then of an outer skin (the rain

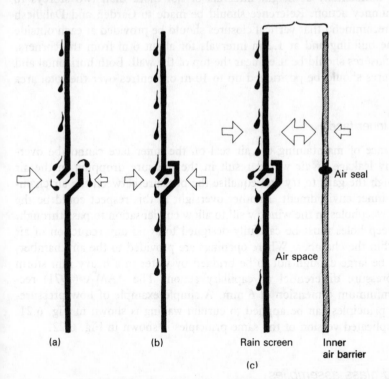

(a)   (b)   Rain screen   Inner
                                     air barrier
              (c)

Fig. 6.20 Essential features of the rain screen and pressure-equalised wall construction (based on AAMA, 1971).

screen) and an inner tight wall with an air space between the two. The pressure equalisation is maintained by not tightly sealing the air space with the outside. The seals on the outer skin are known as the 'deterrent seals' and the seals on the inner skin known as the 'air seals'.

Segmentation of the air space

This is the basic theory. The difficulty in practice is that positive pressures on a façade near the ground are much less than those near the top and those near the centre of a façade are usually greater than those near the corners. Projecting elements, such as column covers, mullions and transoms have their effect on the micro-pressures. A horizontal rail may be subjected to pressure at one end and suction at the other. Air flowing through this member trying to equalise the pressure could have a negative pressure at one end and thus water would be drawn into its joint. An important requirement therefore in the design of the air chamber is that it should not be a large space with a number of widely spaced openings to the outside. Instead it has to be of limited size, subdivided into relatively small areas with ideally only one opening in each compartment to the exterior. If mullion or column covers are used as air chambers, they should be blocked off horizontally at height intervals of not more than two storeys to minimise chimney action. Reference should be made to Garden and Dalgliesh (1968) who recommend that vertical closures should be provided at each outside corner of the building and at 1.2 m intervals for about 6 m from the corners. Horizontal closures should be used near the top of the wall. Both horizontal and vertical closures should be positioned up to 10 m on centres over the total area of the wall.

Air seal on inner face

The importance of maintaining the air seal on the inner face cannot be over-stressed. Any leakage of air would result in the pressure dropping in the air moved through the gaps to try and equalise the pressure between the air chamber and the inner environment. Another oversight in this respect could be the provision of weepholes in the window sill to allow condensation to pass through. Any such weep holes must be carefully designed to avoid any reduction of air pressure within the chamber. Where openings are provided to the air chamber, they should be large enough not to be bridged by water in a heavy rain storm causing a pressure differential or capillary action. The AAMA (1971) recommend a minimum dimension of 6 mm. A simple example of how pressure-equalisation principles can be applied to curtain walling is shown in Fig. 6.21. A more complicated version of the same principles is shown in Fig. 6.22.

Suspended glass assemblies

Pilkingtons' 'suspended glass assembly' using glass as the load-carrying material

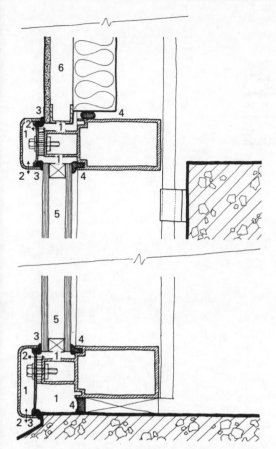

Fig. 6.21 Pressure-equalised standard wall system (vertical section) (based on AAMA, 1971). (1) Pressure-equalised air chamber; (2) Slotted openings; (3) Deterrent seal; (4) Air seal; (5) Hermetically sealed double glazing; (6) Insulated panel.

was first developed with Foster Associates for the Willis, Faber and Dumas Insurance building in Ipswich. The system consists of two glass components: a *wall skin* formed from sheets for 12 mm toughened glass (armourplate) and *vertical fins* fixed perpendicularly to the skin to provide lateral resistance to wind loads. These are formed from 19 mm armourplate.

The system is constructed from the top down. The topmost glass panels are independently suspended from the main structure using one central bolt, the load being spread across the width of the glass by means of a top clamping strip. Figure 6.23 shows the fixing back to the concrete structure at the head of the assembly.

Subsequent panels are hung from those above using 165 mm square brass patch connectors with stainless steel fixing screws. The height of the assembly is limited by the shear strength of the bolt holes that are drilled through the glass, the maximum height being 23 m.

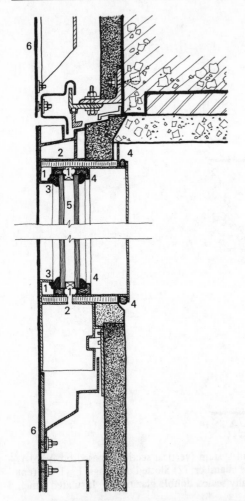

Fig. 6.22   Sketch detail – pressure-equalised wall (based on AAMA, 1971). (1) Pressure-equalised air chamber; (2) Slotted opening; (3) Deterrent seal; (4) Air seal; (5) Hermetically sealed double glazing; (6) Spandrel face.

At Ipswich the glass fin to resist wind loads is fixed back to the floor structure. Since the wall skin is suspended the glass expands downwards. In order to allow vertical movement between the wall and the fin the inside patch connector comes in two parts, one part for attachment to the fin and the other to the façade (see Fig. 6.24). The two parts dovetail together, allowing the fins and façade to slide vertically independently of one another.

The early design of the dovetail, as shown in the Pilkington design guide (1975) included a square dovetail which allowed the two parts of the fin to separate under horizontal movement. Later versions used a rounded sleeve dovetail (see Fig. 6.24). At the base of the assembly, a channel section is fitted which

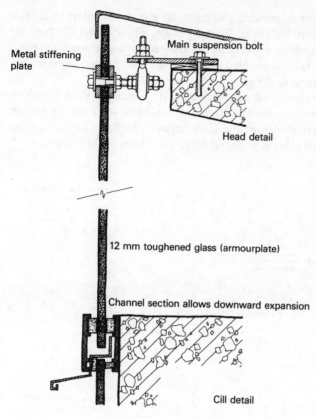

Metal stiffening plate

Main suspension bolt

Head detail

12 mm toughened glass (armourplate)

Channel section allows downward expansion

Cill detail

Fig. 6.23 Method of suspending wall at the Willis, Faber and Dumas building.

supports the glass laterally and has sufficient depth to accommodate the cumulative downward expansion of the façade (see Fig. 6.23).

Joints between the glass are totally exposed to the weather and rely for their efficiency solely on the properties of the silicone-based sealant and the correctness of its application.

The whole system was designed to be capable of accommodating errors in the concrete frame of 50 mm in any direction.

Within ten years Pilkington had reduced the means of securing toughened glass to a flush countersunk machine screw fitting. This fitting known as 'Planar' was first used on Briarcliff House, Farnborough, by Arup Associates and at the Renault Centre by Foster Associates (Fig. 6.25). This was later developed for use with double glazing typically comprising 10mm outer toughened glass, 16mm air space and 6mm inner toughened glass as first used on the Porsche UK Headquarters, Reading by Dewhurst Haslam Partnership in the form of 4° rooflights. These projects relied upon a grid of pick-up points of approximately 2 metre square in order to reduce the deflections between the fittings. The most refined support system for suspended glazing to date is the stainless steel wire wind bracing at Parc de la Villete in Paris by Rice, Francis and Ritchie, for Adrien Fainsiber in 1986 where a special detail allowed a span between the main structure of 8 metre square, and enabled flexing of the wire-braced intermediate structure and also alignment of the glass.

Later (1989) developments of suspended glazing include East Croydon Station by Alan Brookes Associates where cast stainless steel outriggers are used to reduce the effective span of the glass between fittings. Thus the span of the 12 mm toughened glass is reduced from 3000 mm to 2400 mm.

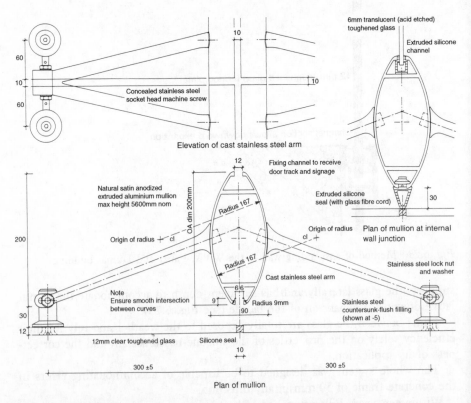

Fig. 6.24 Detail of Aluminium mullion and glazing support at East Croydon Station (architects: Alan Brookes Associates)

The mast is held at its head and base by stainless steel castings with an articulated head detail, to accommodate the vertical and differential movement between the structure and the vertical cladding. The 10 mm clear toughened glass roof glazing is suspended below stainless steel twin armed castings using 902 mark 2 'Planar' fittings.

Fig. 6.25   View of roof glazing suspended below structure at East Croydon Station (courtesy of Chris Grech) (architects: Alan Brookes Associates).

The future of glass assemblies lies not only in investigating a more sophisticated means of environmental control using responsive glazing, but also to develop technology of adhesives superior in mechanical performance to silicones used in current bonded assemblies. The next generation of suspended glazing will take account of the structural properties of the complete assemblies, including the glass, to produce more elegant means of suspension and more economic assembly methods.

References

Architectural Aluminium Manufacturers' Association (1971) *Aluminium Curtain Walls – The Rain Screen Principle and Pressure Equalisation Wall Design*, Feb. 1971, AAMA: New York.

Birkeland, O. (1962) *Curtain Walls*, Handbook 11.B., Norwegian Building Research Institute: Oslo.

British Standards (1977) *Patent glazing*, BS 5516: 1977.

Crawford, D. (1974) 'Design opportunities in patent glazing', *The Architect*, Dec. 1974, pp. 48–50.

Elder, A. J. (1977) *The A. J. Handbook of Building Enclosure*, Architectural Press: London, pp. 151–6.

Frohnsdorff, G. (1981) Proceedings of the second international conference on the durability of building materials and components, 14–16.9.81, National Bureau of Standards, Gaithersburg, Maryland, USA.

Garden, G. K. (1963) *Rain Penetration and its Control*, National Research Council of Canada, Doc. CB D40.

Garden, G. K. and Dalgliesh, W. A. (1968) *Influence of Wind Pressures on Joint Performance*, Technical Paper 264, National Research Council: Canada.

Guedes, P. (1979) *Encyclopedia of Architecture and Technological Change*, 'Glazing systems', Macmillan: London, p. 284.

Hix, J. (1974) *The Glass House*, MIT: Cambridge, Mass., USA.

Hunt, W. D. (1958) *The Contemporary Curtain Wall – Its Design Fabrication and Erection*, F. W. Dodge Corporation: New York.

Patent Glazing Conference (1978) *Patent Glazing – Guidance Notes to BS 5516*, PGC: Epsom, Surrey, March 1978.

Patent Glazing Conference (1980) 'Patent glazing, product selection and specification', *Architects' Journal*, 3.12.1980 (reprints available from PGC, 13, Upper High Street, Epsom, Surrey).

Pilkington Bros. (1975) *Armourplate Suspended Glass Assemblies*, Pilkington design guide, Pilkington Bros. Ltd, St. Helens, Merseyside, Sept 1978.

Rostron, M. (1964) *Light Cladding of Buildings*, Architectural Press: London.

Schaal, R. (1961) *Curtain Walls – Design Manual*, Reinhold: New York.

Stacey, M. 'Products Development – Maximum Vision' *Architects' Journal*, Focus Edition October 1988.

Stroud, Foster and Harington (1979) 'Cladding – curtain walling', *Mitchells Building Construction Structure and Fabric*, 2nd edn, Part 2, Batsford: London pp. 167–75.

Index

Pages on which there are illustrations are indicated in **bold** type.